A HAPPY RHYMER

Selected Works of Anne Sutherland Brooks

Introduced and Selected by Edward Butts

Vocamus Editions
Guelph, Ontario

ISBN 13: 978-1-928171-82-9 (pbk)
ISBN 13: 978-1-928171-83-6 (ebk)

Vocamus Editions
130 Dublin Street, North
Guelph, Ontario, Canada
N1H 4N4

www.vocamus.net

2019

For Christine

Anne Sutherland Brooks

INTRODUCTION

Anne Sutherland Brooks might well be considered one of Canada's lost poets. Original publications of her work are rare outside special collections archives such as those of the University of Guelph's McLaughlin Library and the Metropolitan Toronto Library. Some scholars of Canadian literature might debate the fine point as to whether her work should be classified as poetry or verse, and Anne referred to herself as "a happy rhymer." But humble though Anne was about her art, she nonetheless considered herself a poet, as did colleagues who were also her correspondents. They included such luminaries as Charles G.D. Roberts, Margaret Marshall Saunders, E.J. Pratt, William P. Macdonald, Mazo de la Roche, Lucy Maud Montgomery, and distinguished literary critic William Arthur Deacon.

Anne was born in Guelph, Ontario, on July 24, 1900, the fifth of the six children of John and Annie (née Saunders) Sutherland. She and her siblings: John, James, Mary, Margaret and Robert grew up in a middle-class household in which they were immersed from their earliest years in the wonders of books and the heritage of their pioneering Scottish forebears. By the age of seven Anne had fallen in love with the magic of words and was writing verses and stories inspired by the works of favourite authors such as Lewis Carroll, and everyday happenings in her home.

Anne attended the Guelph Collegiate and – even though her family was Presbyterian – Guelph's Loretto Academy, a convent school for girls operated by Roman Catholic nuns. She then enrolled in Normal School [teacher's college] in London, Ontario. Upon receiving her teacher's certificate, Anne taught for a year in a one-room country schoolhouse in the village of Blair in the county of Waterloo.

When one of Anne's nephews was stricken with poliomyelitis, he was sent to his Sutherland grandparents' home in Guelph to convalesce.

Anne, now in her twenties, began writing stories and verses to entertain him. She submitted some of her work to *The Chatelaine*, a popular women's periodical. The magazine published one of the poems and paid her ten dollars.

That was the beginning of Anne's professional literary career. As Anne Sutherland, she had work published in numerous Canadian periodicals: *The New Outlook, Canadian Forum, The Churchman, The Rainbow, Good Housekeeping, Canadian Magazine* and *The Canadian Bookman* among them. Her work was also published in the United States in various magazines including *American Forests* and *Forest Life*, published by the American Forestry Association in Washington, D.C. Her poems appeared in British publications such as *Essex Countryside*.

In 1927, Lorne Pierce, editor of the prestigious Ryerson Press in Toronto, began introducing young Canadian poets to the reading public. He published their works in collections called chapbooks, a name he borrowed from the old British tradition of printed ballads sold by pedlars. One of Ryerson's first chapbooks was Anne Sutherland's *Within a Wicket Gate*.

The little book formally marked Anne's entry into the wider world of letters. One of the poems, "Poverty," appeared on the editorial page of the *New York Times*. The many letters the *Times* subsequently received indicated that Anne had touched an audience.

Anne Sutherland was now in demand on the public reading circuit. She took to the podium in cities across Ontario as the guest of honour of women's clubs, press clubs and literary organizations. In the coming years she would follow the success of *Within a Wicket Gate* with other chapbooks: *Little Songs for Sale* (1928), *A Ribband of Blue* (1929), *The Sunne-Beam Staire* (1930), *The Odd Little Soul* (1933), *Blue Dusk and Other Poems* (1934), and *I Met Some Little People* (1941). In 1937 she collaborated with her friend and fellow poet Charlotte McCoy on "Sing a Song of Canada," which was put to music.

Anne reached even larger audiences with recitations of her poetry over radio. The rapidly developing new medium carried her voice and words into urban and rural homes across the country. Foster Hewitt, the future legendary voice of Hockey Night in Canada, invited her to tell her children's stories on his program on Toronto's CFCA. Anne called that experience an adventure, but as a teacher she must have been especially delighted to learn that Ontario schoolchildren would see some of her poems in their "readers." Anne Sutherland's work had become part of the educational curriculum, along with that of such noted Canadian poets as Bliss Carmen and William Henry Drummond.

Nathaniel Benson, drama editor for *Saturday Night* magazine, edited an anthology titled *Modern Canadian Poetry* brought out in 1930 by Graphic Publishers of Ottawa. He included six of Anne's poems. On the fly-leaf of the copy Benson presented to Anne he wrote "one of the authentic poets who made my volume possible."

In 1933, Anne's poem "To One Mistaking Little Christ" won the poetry award for the Toronto branch of the Canadian Authors' Association (CAA). A year later her poem "Blue Dusk" earned that award for her again. The year 1934 brought Anne yet another honour when she received a letter from Theodore Roosevelt, Jr., son of the late President of the United States. In recognition of Teddy Roosevelt's efforts to conserve millions of acres of land as national parks and wildlife preserves, the Sears Publishing Company of New York was producing a book called The Roosevelt Bird Sanctuary Anthology. Theodore, Jr. requested and was granted Anne's permission to include her poem, "The Bird I Do Not Know."

Roosevelt wrote to Anne again in 1937. He and his sister, Alice Roosevelt Longworth, were compiling *The Desk Drawer Anthology: Poems for the American People*. That was a collection of poems that had been previously published in periodicals and then submitted to the Roosevelts by readers from across the United States. Out of more than 40,000 submissions, Anne's poem "The Empty Little House" was among the favourites. Theodore and Alice wanted to include it. The only other Canadian poems chosen for the book were Bliss Carmen's "The Joys of the Road" and "The Enchanted Traveller," and John McCrae's "In Flanders Fields."

In 1933, Anne was with the group of thirty men and women of the CAA who toured Great Britain. They visited places of historical and literary interest, and were introduced to Rudyard Kipling, George Bernard Shaw, P.G. Wodehouse and Florence (Dugdale) Hardy, the widow of Thomas Hardy. Upon meeting the Canadians, Shaw quipped that he hadn't known Canada had any authors. The speech Kipling made to the group, in which he said Canadian and British writers shared a common heritage, was recorded and can be heard on YouTube. The CAA party also met Lady Aberdeen, President of the International Council of Women and wife of the former Governor General of Canada; British Prime Minister Ramsay McDonald, and Canadian Prime Minister Richard B. Bennett who was in England to attend a World Economic Council.

In an era in which women tended to marry young, Anne was still single in her early thirties. Then in 1934 she met Edward Arnold Brooks, a clergyman who was an assistant to the pastor of St. George's Anglican Church in Guelph. Born in Simcoe, Ontario, Brooks was seven years younger than Anne, but neither the difference in age nor religious affiliations stood in the way of blossoming romance. They were married in Toronto on April 30, 1935. Brooks generally went by his second name, although family and friends often addressed him as "Canon." Anne affectionately called him "The Hunter." Their son John Edward Arnold was born in 1937, and in 1943 they adopted a baby girl, Anne Elizabeth. From the time of her marriage, Anne wrote under the name Anne Sutherland Brooks.

Arnold's calling required him to move his family from one assigned parish to another. They lived in Guelph, Hamilton and Acton before Arnold was sent to St. Andrew's Church in Grimsby in 1944. That community would be their home for the next twenty years.

For much of that period, Anne devoted her time to being a mother and a rector's wife. She was active in parish women's groups, but continued to write, still finding inspiration in everyday family life. Then in 1949 she was diagnosed with spinal tuberculosis and was sent to a sanitarium in Hamilton. She didn't return home until 1951.

In 1964-65 Anne and Arnold spent a year touring Great Britain. As Anne had done three decades earlier, they visited historic sites and made friends with people in every little community they passed through. Arnold had the opportunity to be guest speaker at services in centuries-old churches. During yet another trip to Britain a few years later, Anne and Arnold made a pilgrimage to the ancestral home of the Sutherland clan in Scotland.

After Grimsby, Anne and Arnold lived in Jarvis, Ontario, and then Hamilton. In her later years, Anne found a new outlet for artistic expression – painting. But she never stopped writing. She composed verses for her grandchildren and worked on a journal. In 1984 she published *Not Now ... Then*. The book is an autobiography that outlines her career as a writer and provides insights into the real-life stories behind many of her poems. It is also a travelogue of her trips to Great Britain, full of her observations on history, literature, and men and women of legend. It includes several previously unpublished poems.

Arnold passed away on November 21, 1993. Anne followed him on January 8, 1996. They are buried together in the cemetery of St. Andrew's Church in Grimsby.

By the time of Anne's death her work had long been out of print. Her name was mentioned in passing or in footnotes in bibliographic studies of Canadian poetry, but she had otherwise been forgotten. In this book, readers once again have the opportunity to experience Anne's work.

Much of what Anne wrote was for children. Her most whimsical verses are laced with the magic and innocence of childhood in domestic settings that are still relevant a century after they were written. Her verses show the influence of A.A. Milne's Winnie-the-Pooh stories and Robert Louis Stevenson's *A Child's Garden of Verses*, but the work is nonetheless distinctively Anne's. In the words of one contemporary reviewer, "Such poems as 'The Tinker Fairy' and 'The Toys That Are Left Out Nights' ... bear the quality of fragile delicacy and the imprint of a deep love of childhood that always characterized Mrs. Brooks' writings."

A significant portion of Anne's poetry reflects her devout Christian faith. She shines through her work as a humanist with a great sensitivity for the cares and struggles of people everywhere. Anne was also profoundly moved by the wonders of nature, the seasons, gardens, the creatures of fantasy, and the works of poets and novelists whom she considered giants of English literature. The mature insight of Anne's poems created on those themes makes them stand apart from her verses for children and her devotional celebrations.

Unique among Anne's published work – and indeed, in Canadian literature – is *The Odd Little Soul*. In this work of prose, written at the time of her nephew's illness, a narrator (Anne) paints an introspective, anecdotal picture of daily events in a real-life household. Most of the characters are the children of Anne's own extended family. They and the few adults with whom they interact are identified through nicknames that match their personalities. Among them are John-Make-a-Dream, the Doctor, Miss Sagacity, Polly Comfort, the General Manager, Janet Muffin and the Born Agitator.

The narrator's words provide a window into the world of innocent, inquisitive and sometimes reactionary young souls. That world is at once both commonplace and magical, spiced with humour and pathos. Anne's presentation tells the reader much about the author and the time in which she wrote.

This book offers readers but a selection of the work that made Anne Sutherland Brooks a poet of note in her day, with the hope that it will help to re-establish her in a rightful place in Canadian literature.

Edward Butts
Guelph, Ontario
January 2019

POEMS

Invitation

Mine is a humble garden,
And beauty is not rare;
Who is not blind to blossoms
May find them anywhere.

Mine is a gentle mission,
To tend the little gate
And offer rest and comfort
To travellers who wait.

Not you who walk the Highway
From hour to weary hour
Have need of tender birdsong,
Have need of fragrant flower.

And if one rose were wasted
That you, perhaps, should see
How should I face the Owner
Who gave the keys to me?

Sylvan

When they were making these woods I guess
The oldest grey angel sat
Holding a basket of loveliness
And handing out this and that.

Other grey angels moved here and there
And never grew tired or cross,
Scattering seed where the ground was bare,
Knitting the soft, snug moss.

Teaching the bobolink his turn,
Dipping the grass in green,
Sewing the fringes along a fern
With little black knots between.

Gilding the fragile butterfly,
Scenting the forest air,
Sometimes, smiling, happening by
The little round hillock where,

Scissors in hand, with anxious brow,
The little white angel lay
Prostrate beneath a shady bough,
Cutting out leaves all day.

February Night

When the Wind came into the forest
That blustery, blustery night,
A Star stumbled down in the dark with
A light;
The young Trees huddled together
In whispery, whispery glee;
The old Trees never awakened
To see
Why the floor of the forest should creak with
That shivery, shivery sound,
Strange bodiless grey things went dancing
Around;
Then the Littlest Tree in the forest

Grew frightened, frightened, and so
He got right down under his blanket
Of snow.

The Mystic

I to the dull am brain,
I to the weak am brawn,
I to the drouth am rain,
I to the storm am Dawn.

I am the perfume of the rose,
I am the glory of the star,
I am the flame that men suppose
Is the sunrise in the east afar,
I am the smile on the lips that sleep,
I am sweet in the eyes that weep,
I am in birth and death, I ween,
And all along the road between.

I to the knight his spur, I to the nun her beads,
I to the wayfarer
All that a pilgrim needs
I am the fleet doe on the hill,
I am as young as a madcap Pan,
I am despaired of hunter's skill,
I have teased since the world began,
And each has a part, but none the whole –
I will be chained to no man's soul.
Hearts have no gold without alloy;
Seek not to keep me – I am Joy!

Early April

There's a cold, cold wind and a leaden sky
And a drift of dirty snow,
And you'd never dream that the draggled sod
Had a crocus hid below.
There's the dreary sob of the dripping branch
But never a song is heard,
And the little wee tenantless house in the tree

Is wanting a master bird.
But hark! Oh hark! From the far, far hills
There's a sweet, sweet piercing ring –
'Tis the wild, weird call of the pipes o' Pan
And they're summoning in the Spring.

Ah, who'd resist? For the life-blood stirs
With the stir of sap in the bough,
And the dream of fruiting that woke the tree
Is creeping to blossom now;
There's a throbbing pulse to the fragrant air
And the brook breaks free to run,
While the little Earth, singing her paean of birth,
Is smiling back at the sun,
And hark! hark! hark! from the far, far hills
There's a sweet, sweet piercing ring,
'Tis the wild, weird call of the pipes o' Pan
And they're summoning in the Spring.

Youth

Like silver icicles strung on a slender bough,
The shining years go by for me;
I am so beauty-rapt I touch them now
Almost worshipfully.

When, wise-eyed, I shall hold them in my eager hand,
But newly-broke for my desire
To search their beauty and to understand
How ice is blent with fire,

Shall I still find them lovely as I find them now,
With the dear joy of wondering gone,
Or shall I wish them back upon the bough,
Luring my fingers on?

Au Revoir to Winter

What means this happy whispering
Within my garden walls,
The little folk all donning

Their gayest fol-de-rols,
A Robin Redbreast swaggering
About the oozy lawn?
It is a farewell party
Ere winter shall have gone!

Old Sol, in golden livery,
Attends the joyful guests;
The Trees are decked with silver
And carry little nests;
Miss Sky wears azure crepe-de-chine
With scarf of ostrich tips;
The debutantes, slim Tulips,
Flaunt carmine on their lips;

Pan, with his winged orchestra,
Is hidden in the trees,
And oh! The wild, sweet music
That trembles on the breeze,
While through the madcap revelry
A drift of glinting snow,
Like silver-dipt confetti,
Dusts up the scene below.I shall not go to frolic there,
For I could not forget
That just outside my garden
A Wren and Violet,
The little new acquaintances,
Stand wistfully and wait
For sunny Spring to bring them
Within the garden gate.

Poverty

I met her on the street today and she
Just turned her lovely eyes away from me.

But ah! I can forgive her, for I know,
If she seems dull, what things have made her so.
She is so closely wrapped in costly fur,
No tingling wind has ever quickened her;
She never felt warm rain upon her face,

(Her motor takes her round from place to place)
That slender hand, bright with its jewelled ring,
Has never searched the sweet damp earth in Spring
For little growing things; nor have those eyes
Been tender with the light of sacrifice;
She may not laugh nor weep nor cry aloud
(The vogue is to be blasé in her crowd):
She thrills not to the promise of the Dawn,
She greets the hush of starlight with a yawn,
And Life has sheltered her, poor thing!
From all the holy joy of suffering.

Resurrection

I think, if there had been no Easter morn,
There'd be no April now,
A sombre lethargy would lie upon
The meadow and the bough.
What robinsong could fill the awesome hush
Of Wounded faith – of loss?
What tree lift up her proud and leafy head
Whose branch had been His Cross?
What violets ecstatically spring
To sunshine and to bloom
Whose hearts would lie, like His Who fashioned them,
Each in its small dark tomb?

Or little waters laugh and croon again
Their raptured songs at will,
When that dear Voice that bades them leap and flow
Would be – forever – still?

Death, but not mating, in the last year's nest,
Thorns, but not blossoms, on the bough, -
I think, if there had been no Easter morn,
There'd be no April now.

The Lecture

It's very trying; here am I
Endeavoring to find out why

(From this Professor Know-What's-What)
Some verse is good and some is not.
I look attentive, I am sure;
My countenance is most demure,
My feet set primly side by side,
My telltale mouth most dignified,
But I shall never learnedly
Discuss poetic symmetry,
And I shall never, never scan
As fast as this Professor man!
I feel he would be very sad
To see the scribbles on my pad
And know his Stentor voice was drowned
In such a tiny, crooning sound,
But close outside the window-pane,
With all his tender might and main,
A small Professor in a tree
Is *singing* poetry to me.

The Transients

God give me magnanimity when they are in the wrong
And help me drown my anger in the busyness of song –
Alas! I shall not have their foolish ways to hurt me long.

Or, if they speak unkind to me and I would answer ill,
Pray Heaven check my eager tongue and discipline my will
To search the foolish heart of me and find I love them still,

For when, the new Day dawned for them on every gilt-edged tree,
They start upon the shining trail with mirth and minstrelsy,
You know there will be pain enough – without remorse for me!

Leaves

Leaves be most lovable in bud,
Born in a morn of May,
Pink-cheeked with baby zeal to push the swaddling-clothes away,
They hang the world in blossom long before the blossom day.

And green leaves lie so drowsily
Upon a tree's curved breast,
And make so gentle music they can lull a soul to rest –
Oh, since His word be weary-worn, God knew the green was best.

But I love nights of witchery
When trees grow twice more high
And leaves that have been rose and green while Springtime days went by
And black silk tatters fretting there against a silver sky.

Mary, The Mother

When Jesus Christ hung crucified
One knew his Captain dead
And all the battle yet unwon
And bitter the days ahead,
And one, who had been blind before,
Was given his sight to see
The loved Physician suffering there
On Merciless Calvary;
And one, a woman, beat her breast
And called on Heaven to save
Her Saviour, and a rich man went
To make his King a grave.

But Mary, the Mother, only wept
For a little Boy Who'd lain
When he was five, against her breast,
And cold His grave, small pain,
And mourned, as every mother must mourn,
For the little Boy Who'd grown
So tall and strong and brave and wise
He could bear His hurt alone.

A Tree

Were I to choose, I'd like to be
A green old tree.
I'd like to reach up very high
To touch the soft blue sky
And yet to keep my humble feet

In a grey city street.
In blossom-time I'd be by grace
A wayside holy place
And shake my silly fragrance down
On all the passing town.

If one green pathway to the sky
Grew tiresome, couldn't I
Send out a slim grey branch to be
A brand-new path for me?
All day I'd spin my golden dreams
From little broke sunbeams;
At dusk I'd watch the Lady Moon
Put on her silver shoon,
And ah! So far from yielding breath
To a grey sad-eyed Death,
How glorious when I was old
To burn away in gold!

Even I, who have not touched the sky,
Can understand just why
An acorn works so hard to be
An old green tree.

Enquiry

Would you be a red rose,
Flaunting in the sun,
Knowing all the world yours
For its homage won?

Would you be a white rose,
Weary, weary, wise,
Knowing all there is to know
But how a rose dies?

Or would you be a young bud
On a green wing,
Toppling on the garden wall
Drunk with venturing?

Hyacinths

The pride of little windows when they be
Holding pink hyacinths for us to see!

"Lord God!" said Valentine, that kindly saint,
"Vittoria's golden voice is silent now,
Enraptured with the feast of music here
He sits and listens to the seraphim;
Anselmo brews his potent herbs no more,
Heaven hath no need of healing medicine,
And Angelo is prostate at the shrine
Of her whose face he oft had tried to paint.
All are content but Valentine – Lord God,
Forgive – these hands of mine, grown used on earth
To the performance of small services,
Are idle now, and idle, discontent.
Could'st Thou not find some little task of Thine
That could be given to humble Valentine?"

Oh, gently then the Lord God smiled and gave
Into the hands of Valentine a charge
That brings contentment to the good saint's heart.
Soon as the brilliant February sun
Pours down its golden warmth upon the earth,
Row upon row of little stout brown bulbs
Old Valentine takes from their shelf in Heaven,
And with his thumb-nail digs a hole in each
And breathes therein his tender messages
And seals them with his lips, and in the night,
When all the harps are silent, softly goes
To the great gate of Heaven and there commends
His Valentines unto the ministry
Of earth and rain and sun and you and me.

Then all the windows of the world, God wot,
Are glad that Valentine has not forgot.

Easter (In a Florist's Window)

Scarlet is dripping here, bright like the blood of Him;
Dull red of shame for the brow that betrayed:

Yellow of daffodil sheathed in its green, the thing
Mockers held up to Him, taunted Him, made
Jest to his agony.

April's own joyful blue,
This, ere the darkness fell, this was the sky,
(And, perhaps, matinsong? Flaunting ecstatic wings
Close to the Cross when Springtime passed by?)

Tender brown petals – nay, nay, they are human
Crucified eyes as He whispered, "Befriend,
Loved of disciples, my Mother." Ah, Son of Man!
This is Your going then. This is the end.

Purple of pansies to mourn for a King of kings,
Silvery grey of the tulips with tears
Misting their mauve, and a violet, child of the
Garden of Arimathea and years.

Blend in the April dusk scarlet and saffron hue,
Fades the swift vision. Gethsemane come and gone.
Then, in the startled gloom, tired, glorified, His Face,
A single lily-bloom.
        As it began to dawn ...

Perspective

An artist splashed on a window-pane
A green, a blue and a crimson stain,
A bluebird stared with his beady eye
And called to a June bug crawling by,
"The world has come to a pretty pass
When grapes grow out of a window-glass!"

The June bug looked much mystified,
He climbed the glass and he peered inside,
Then his little brown body shook with mirth
And he cried, "You're right. It's a funny old earth,
And you're the fellow to know, because
I see *you* live on a china vase!"

11

L'Improvvisatore

It matters not how misty grey the sky,
How dully grey the sea,
I need but turn my head and lift my eye,
And lo! white wings for me.

It matters not how grimy brown the field,
How slimy deep the swale,
I need but stoop to find the grasses yield
White blossoms, pure and frail,

And curtained though in grey obscurity
The mind's high journeys seem,
I search along some hidden fold and see
A silver edge of Dream.

Song of Summer's End

Gypsy feet, you must travel far
From dusky forest and hill o'dream,
Bid good-bye to blossom and star,
Laughing water and sunset gleam;
(But, primly walking in shoes of leather,
You'll dream of the lanes we tramped together!)

Small brown hands, there are less-loved parts
Than building pillows of soft pine-needles,
Weaving dreams where the sleek trout darts,
Strewing crumbs where a brown bird wheedles,
(Some time you'll tire of paper and pen,
And then you'll dream of a brook again!)

Little gay heart, when the world's way palls
And paths of custom grow dull and drear,
Come in dreams where the brown bird calls,
And stars and angels are near!
(When daisies bloom and the dawn's at seven
Gypsy paths are the nearest Heaven!)

October

Dull silver streams of cloud o'erspread the sky,
And from the West a rough, young, tyrant breeze
Comes whirling down my garden path and whips
Their tattered garments round the shrinking trees;
Blown seed and wasted bud and birdsong stilled,
The dancing days of leaf and sunbeam done,
And where October's ruthless hand has swept
Frail silken wing and crumpled rose are one.

Sweet Summer, drooping by the garden wall,
Lifts up again her lovely greying head
In one last glorious attempt to live,
Ere, on her wounded breast, slow bloodstains spread;
A mist of tears obscures her from my sight,
The silver wings of Death, descending, shine,
And lo! where Summer lay – a crumbling wall
Stained with the crimson of a tangled vine.

Invocation at the Year's Passing

O weep not that this leaf be spoiled
Like all the others turned before,
And thou can'st work with it no more;
But hand it in all rubbed and soiled,

And know the Great Examiner,
When He thy labored script has scanned,
Will lay it gently from His Hand
And say, " 'Twas no light task for her."

He knew when teardrops uncontrolled
Spread on the page an ugly blot,
When weariness fell to thy lot
And made the pen a weight to hold,

And He is gentler than we think
When Sin holds out too strong a lure,
And fingers that He hoped were pure
Go trailing through the scarlet ink.

A virgin page He offers here;
Then dry thine eyes and humbly ask
That He will oversee thy task,
And face it, unrestrained by fear:

But write with care, remembering this,
Remorse may seize the erring pen
If, when He turns the page again,
Thou findest written there – FINIS.

L'Envoi

I would go out of a garden,
Closing the gate
Softly, lest in the gloaming
Some little late
Lover, brown-feathered, desiring
Share in a nest,
Startles, should fly away; or in
The meek, lovely breast
Of the white rose there'd be sorrow
That I had gone,
Or lest a butterfly waken,
Thinking it Dawn.

I would take leave of a garden
Gently, and then
I should be sure of a welcome
Again.

Guelph – Our Heritage

Anne Sutherland read the following poem on April 23, 1927, at a luncheon following a tree planting ceremony in Priory Square, Guelph, as part of the city's centennial celebration.

O little Royal City! When
Our grandsires dreamed you, long ago
They could not guess the wilderness,
Where ring of axe and sturdy blow

Of hammer woke the solemn hush
And split with silver streaks the green,
Should temper strength with tenderness
And make a cradle for a queen!
Our fathers – honor to their names! –
Took up the task with ready heart,
Built, shaped, perfected, used with skill
Their ken of science, commerce, art,
And dropped for us the fertile seed
Within the eager virgin sod
And died, bequeathing us their dream,
To build a city to their God.
Liege lady! Loyally today
We come – devoted native sons
And, pinning laurels on your brow,
These others, the adopted ones,
And, homesick for your blessing, link
Our hearts about your heart and find
Still in your queenly role you keep
What treasures we have left behind,
Whate'er your children knew and loved,
Like flowers in your gracious hold,
The little dear familiar paths,
The schoolhouse where we went of old,
The church, the family pew, the stained
Glass window of our child amaze,
The cottage garden and the creek
We fished and swam in boyhood days,
The company of friends who wait
To clasp our hands for auld lang syne
And share the cup and sing the songs
Of you and yours and me and mine;
And nearest to her throbbing heart
Our own and hers who silent lie
In their eternal lovely sleep.
Most gracious sovereign city! We
In loving homage gather. Take
Us back into your heart, we pray
Centennial morn, for Old sake's sake.

The Vendor of Songs

My shelves are filled with little songs
Of hope and trust and cheer,
I sing them at the open door
For all the world to hear,
I sell them for a penny or
A prayer or a smile,
I give a sample song away
Every little while.

I make my little friendly songs
Of all the things I see,
I found one in a daffodil,
I heard one from a bee,
I wove one out of little winds,
I caught one in the rain,
I piped one out of laughter and
Stitched one out of pain.

And if I rode the grey clouds
Before the Dawn was red,
I'd pull a little song of stars
Round about my head,
And if I had the King's crown
I'd hammer it apart,
If I could hear the faintest hum
From its shining heart!

First Glow

All things but just begun I love; the prelude to a song;
The little eager waking buds upon an April tree;
A hushed "Our Father" heralding petition, free and strong;
The curve of road that bears my heart along ahead of me;
Dear, shy, small Dawn that strews her path with roses for the day;
A brown field freshly-furrowed and a cosy waiting nest;
First rosebud for the centre of a pretty prim bouquet;
A very little baby and an altar newly-blest.

There's nothing left but praise or blame for what is nearly done,
But oh! the sweet o'dreaming on the thing that's just begun.

16

The Little Botanist

I like to walk with Patrick
On a summer day,
For Patrick talks of wild flowers
In the sweetest way,
Old ladies' clothespins,
Scarlet wickawee,
Rough Joe-pye-weed,
Woodbetony,
Old man's pepper,
Lady-never-fade,
Gayfeather in the sun,
Hyssop in the shade,
Blue witch's thimble and
Yellow touch-me-not,
Roosterhead and candlewick
In a marshy spot.
Patrick says "Masther Bob,"
And the flower bends,
And I take off my cap,
And faith we're friends!

The Diligents

Madrigal on my lips ... Wings in her sky,
We are very happy, April and I.

April has – oh, how many! – new little tasks,
The corners of clouds are grimy and the road basks
In a sweet somnolence; lilacs must hang out bloom;
Nests be fashioned and feathered, and the shut room
Of the forest be opened with scamper and song.
April is anxious that nothing at all go wrong.

And I have a basket to line, a ribbon to run,
The house to be kept ready, the mending done,
And a shawl and a little blue bassinet to buy.
We are very happy, April and I.

Valentine

He said:
"Thank God those days when sentiment
Ran awry are disposed of, and I've come
To see you, not in satin, frills of lace
About my wrists, my head bowed down with some
Top-heavy structure, powdered, tied with blue
Silk ribbons. And I do not bend and kiss
Your fingertips and bore you with a long
Poetic dissertation how there's this
And this about you I admire, because
We are companions mentally. You know
I like you and I need not tell you so."

And I replied (and yawned behind my hand)
"It's always been a mystery to me
How persons of intelligence could stand
Their trite affected gestures. Obviously
Our ancestors thought Life was lovelier
For being swathed in eider and in rose.
They lacked our courage; we have stripped Life bare
And still we love it. Pity, pity those
Poor mid-Victorian blind!"
And then he left,
And I unwrapped his gift and – well, I cried.
There were forget-me-nots inside.

The Bairnie O' The Clan

O small beloved Chieftain,
Your ancestors were men
Who piped their stormy pibroch
And fought from glen to glen;
Yet you come down among us,
As little and as fair
As some white sprig o' heather
But newly-blossomed there,
Your stronghold but a cradle,
And you, oh little laddie,
Dear helpless monarch sleeping there,
With blankets for your plaidie!

Our hearts go down before you,
Whose wee clenched fist must hold
So much of hard-earned treasure
Within its petal-fold
No paltry hoard of riches,
No passing meed of fame,
But beautiful and lasting,
The honour of your name:
God point you, little Chieftain,
The road your grandsires ran,
And give His tenderest blessing to
The bairnie o' the Clan!

Centennial

A city grows more lovely growing old.
Her raw red structures in the sun of years
Fade mellowly to rose and wreath themselves
In ivy. Birds come back to nestle there
Spring after Spring. Grey stones are beaten smooth
And kindly with the hammering of rain.
God's Acre feels the fingers of the moss
Creep tenderly above her sleeping dead
And bandages the scars upon her sod
With shining myrtle and with ribbon-grass.
The Sabbath morn is intimate with bells
And touches them in reverential joy,
For thus and so their spirits have communed
Through years and happy years. The flag that rides
Atop the gale is old with many storms
And proud with history. And all the hills
That girdle with their ribbonings of green
A greying city, bend them and are filled
With echoes of her songs. Her gracious lap
Is heaped with prosper and her heart is big
With faith and affection. Memory
Walks with her in twilight and at Dawn
Comes Hope and shines serenely from her brow.

Like lace and lavender and filigree
Of silver, like the scent of potpourri

And like a tale a hundred times retold
A city grows more lovely growing old.

The Quaker Bride

Quoth she, and hid her shining eyes,
"Tomorrow early I will rise
And careful lay these clothes away
And garb me for my wedding-day:
A gown of patience finely sewn,
A fichu stitched in faith alone,
A cloak of courage and a hood
Of modesty –" The crimson flood
Ran o'er her cheek "-and- save me now!-
This wreath of rapture on my brow –"
 And truth, when on the morn she went
To pledge her bridal sacrament,
Thee never saw a Royal Maid
More fitly clad, more fair arrayed.

Nocturne

Let me grow tired as flowers grow tired
Who spend their fragrance recklessly
For every vagrant fingertip
And waste their substance on a bee.
Let me have need as stars have need
Of that deep-bosomed tranquil breast
Of Night, to cool this fevered brow
When I have given my trembling best.
Dawn will break soon enough and wings
From every hawthorn flash and start,
Now let us lie as hushed birds lie
Whom love keeps silent, heart to heart –

All things that shine and dance and bloom
And hurt their slender throats to sing,
Night waits in her dear darkling room,
Their tiredness is a lovely thing.

Philosophy On Gardens

A little, old garden has a very special grace.
Who'd deny a daisy's begging? Who'd resist a pansy-face?
Shut his heart to sweet alyssum where it creeps and whitens? Who,
In the fragrance of a lily, feels not prayer rising too?
Something in the way verbenas crowd and blossom; hollyhocks
Lift their quaint bright sunshades over candytuft and fairy phlox,
How the golden-glow and larkspur stand up bravely to the Dawn,
Build the white and purple bells a Canterbury carillon, -
Ah, it tangles round your heartstrings, like the fern and ribbon-grass
Reaches out and plucks and stays you when you try to pass.

A very large garden is a little frightening,
And its flower-names, you'll find, have a sophisticated ring;
Fancy bending down to touch and love a *myosotis*. Yet
In little gardens it's the bloom that bids you not forget!

Then the *primula vulgaris* might be shocked to have you know
She was little English primrose that you used to cherish so!
Not a single lady's bonnet! No old man in chummy nooks
Or bachelor's buttons! Only blossoms from the learned books,
Botanists may revel here, but poets, lovers, you and I,
We will doff our hats and curtsey. We will hurry by.

A brand-new garden is so very stiff and staid.
Little ragged buttercups have never wandered here and played;
The columbine is timid and the marigolds are prim,
Sweet William minds his etiquette and grieves the soul of him;
The foxgloves and gaillardias stand frozenly apart,
And with sentiment passé you couldn't find a bleeding heart!
Oh, its stones are grim and whitewashed and its gate is new and green,
And its geometric paths are smooth and pitifully clean,
It has need of love and laughter, foot-prints, voices, night-time, God,
And of April heaped on April to the blessing of the sod.

But a little old garden with a quaint dignity,
Full of colour, sunshine, living, gay with camaraderie,
With the healing of the moss upon its pathway, beckoning
Little lost and ancient blossoms to its breast and sheltering
Wren and robin – here is altar, tryst and sanctuary; here
Come a-homing love and mirth and meditation, faith and cheer;

With the benison of time upon its kindly furrowed face,
Oh, a little old garden has a very special grace!

Miracle

Not here, the miracle,
Because a ship, full-panoplied in all
The majesty of might rides out alone
Upon a monster sea, nor heeds the fall
Of giant force against her. They have thrown
Together, as the sea has taught them to,
A timber and a rigging and a screw
And lo! the ship is here, a complex scheme,
A marvel, a solution and a dream
But not a miracle.

Nor yet a miracle,
Because a city of a million souls
Has come together on a sloping plain,
For so the cave-race dug and shaped their holes
And housed a deal of happiness and pain
Within them; lived and died and left behind
For monument another of their kind.
A city! – yea, a wondrous complex scheme,
A marvel, a solution and a dream
But not a miracle.

For I have searched the desert and the red
Round rim of sunset, and the hidden bed
Of ocean, and the deep caves, and the high
Clean strata of the wide and lustrous sky,
And I have found
Where man has planned and executed much,
Yet lacked the one divinely tender touch
That wove a crown of petals round about
A daisy-head and drew it gently out
Above the ground,
Or in the Spring's sweet silences unwound
A shuttle filled with song and trailed it round
The happy garden. Lo, what else I see
Is only half a miracle to me.

Confessional

He who goes into a forest
Under the burden of care,
Trees shall bend softly and lay their
Light hands on his hair,
Shadow and shelter and silence
Solace him there.

Yea, into the forest cathedral
Scarlet with sin though he go,
Trees shall stoop to forgive him
And bless him, and lo!
He shall go forth into sunlight
Whiter than snow.

Ambush

Who happens on my garden
He finds him special things,
For all the air is joyous
With scarlet wings
Red breasts against the grey walls
And song to charm the ear,
For every passing pilgrim
Some meed of cheer.
So happy they who wander,
So happy they who wait,
That no one scales the grey walls
Or tries the gate
To find the one shy white bird
Within the greenest tree
Whose little hushed heart hopes for
Discovery.

Explorer's Litany

Father in Heaven Who read today to me
A deep and beautiful new litany,
I thank Thee for the undiscovered things,
For lonely, lovely flowers; wanton wings

Above uncharted spaces; trees that keep
A proud reserve of beauty; fish that leap
Unhurt, untroubled, in an unnamed stream;
Hills that are grey and silent with old dream;
For every fragrant hidden honeycomb;
For every rock that roofs a busy home
Of spiders; for the green and lazy snake
That slides among unparted grasses, take
My gratitude; for all untrodden ways,
Undesecrated soil I give thee praise;
For wasted song, ungathered peace, and bold
Uncaptured canvases of pearl and gold,
All Thou had'st kept – untouched – untold –
For me,
Father, I thank Thee!

To a Materialist

I could show you the haunts of the Little People,
Old as the hills and quaint as a wishing-well,
Fairy under the thorn-bush, elves by moonlight,
Wee brown fellow hid in the heather-bell.
Here is the tiny track of their careless making
Here is their silver palace in the grass,
Here, if you looked, a pixie's pointed slipper,
Caught in a leaf-net, dangles where you pass.
What does it matter? You, with your clumsy footstep,
How could you ever hope to find the way?
You, when the lacy fragrant blossom-bridal
Breaks, who will simply stare and call it May.
You who walk in a forest and never listen,
You who come on a toadstool and dare not smile,
But you are dull and trite and somewhat stupid!
I shall go out and leave you afterwhile,
Selfish-glad that your lantern may not find me,
Glad that the valleys shudder when you call –
Why should the darling whimsy Little People
Have to be wearied with you, after all?

An Old Woman

She is a little body, brown and sere,
Like dried wheat in the harvest of the year,
With wrinkled cheeks and faded, sad old eyes
And lips at once both innocent and wise;
Her dress is shabby black and shows no grace
Of ribbon, frill or delicate old lace;
Her feet are bulging with their tired good-will,
Her hands pathetically worn – and still –
And all her countenance bespeaks a mind
Inured to Fate and humble and resigned.

Yet – do not pity her should you pass by;
She is as well-endowed as you or I.
She has – wrapt carefully and hid away –
Her proud old sorrow of another day,
As beautiful a thing in lavender
As you or I could ever furnish her.

Rejection

I'd rather weave a daisy-chain upon a dewy morning,
Lying deep in meadow-grass against a friendly boulder.
Than bandy silly strings of words where costlier suns were burning,
Painted laughter on my lips and orchids at my shoulder.

I'd rather wear the halo that a moon had set upon me
(Point a silver patteran to hush a gypsy hunger),
Than shackle down my eager brow with jewels that had won me
Nothing but the curses of a wild-eyed costermonger!

Red berries for my provender and mosses for my resting –
Poor my silly neighbor whose gold can only buy him
Fashionable haunts of men where, friendship loud protesting,
Iscariot waits for some dark Dawn thrice haply to deny him!

Starting School

God bless a little boy who goes to school,
His shiny Primer hugged against his breast,

With cheeks scrubbed clean and in his rounded eyes
A baby wonder of the strange new quest!
September, take him gently; he is small,
Whose sturdy form must battle with the blow
Of morning: make the red-gold leaves that fall
A carpet where such little feet may go
In safety. Sun, shine tenderly upon
The forehead where his mother laid her kiss.
It was a consecration: see that books
May never rob her little son of this.
Birds, sing him softly; he has only known
A lullaby; and little brook run clear
When he is watching; never let him know
A stagnant secret; he is young and dear.
Pray that he find within the strange four walls
The smile close kin of tears, the heart grown wise
In love of simple things, the hand that shields,
And laughter, laughter, in the waiting eyes.
He was a baby yesterday; he lived
By just my simple rote and easy rule:
There – he is gone, around the curve of road –
Oh! God bless little boys who go to school!

Chloe Is Gone

The room she left is dusty, and the blind
Half-drawn as if she meant to come and find
The sun still waiting. All the little lights
Are patient lest she want them still o' nights.
The pictures glimmer dimly from the wall
Because she hung them there and loved them all,
And every chair in hushed expectancy
Makes cradle for her comfort eagerly:
And oh! though they have seen her turn and go,
The shut piano wants her fingers so
And patiently and hopeful all day long
Holds up her best-loved song.

The Younger Pilgrim

I shall not mind the last years
If only I may be
Proud keeper of the treasure
The first years brought to me.

O heart of mine, if silver
Have never dulled to grey,
If I have cherished laughter,
Not frittered faith away,

If I remember starshine
And keep a tryst with prayer,
Though all my limbs be shaken
I shall not even care;

I shall not ever question,
Nor grumble of my load,
If God but leave His pilgrim
The hunger for the road!

Isolate

My friend, for things that I have hid from you
I ask forgiveness. He who said that all
Truths lay revealed to friendship's clear-eyed gaze
Was wrong; for every man there is a wall
No foot may scale, a gate no hand may force,
An ecstasy no heart can hope to share –
For every soul some time a dol'rous way
And only passage for one pilgrim there.
I have a song I was too shy to sing;
I have a sin I could not let you see;
I have traversed a soil so consecrate
Not even you might venture there with me.
So give your lenience to my stranger mood:
Shall not our friendship take a larger girth?
This is not I, but the Divine in me,
Passing His season on a friendless earth.

Salvia Splendens

Once, in the long ago, under the harvest moon,
Spreading pale golden sheen over dusky glades,
Two brawny red-skinned braves, fired by a maiden's smile,
By her black flashing eyes and her sleek braided hair,
Shed blood upon the soil, red blood on the clean soil.
So hot with rage it was, red-hot with love and rage,
Life in it grew and grew, burst into blossoms red,
Bright as the blood they shed, bright as her laughing lips,
Blossoms of love and rage!

Cool is this autumn night, passionless, still and cool –
No little homing wing dips in the lonely sky;
All the sweet flower-things, crushed, clammy, desolate,
Sprawl in their death-like sleep on the earth's quiet breast.
But, when the harvest moon glimmers all goldenly
Down on the garden wall, gorgeously frescoed there,
On the grey dingy stone salvia blossoms blaze,
Red as a maiden's lips, hot as a young brave's blood,
Blossoms of love and rage!

Leaf-Envy

I've often thought the little leaves
Were luckier than we.
I know it's true that April finds
Them tied upon the tree
In prim green rows, with dainty toes
All uniformly met,
To measured time performing their
Attentive minuet.

But when October winds are high
And take their toll of trees,
The lucky little leaves may do
Exactly as they please.
No need to care what others wear,
Away with proper green,
It's time the personalities
Of eager leaves be seen!

28

Then scarlet leaves can burn away
And russet leaves can lie
Drunk on October's nectared sun,
And gold can dance. But I,
All down the sweet, mad windswept street,
Oh, what am I to do,
Who underneath my careful green
Am gold and scarlet too?

Profaned

Grief came to me a year ago,
When I was insolent with youth.
I met her with a jest; I poured
My laughter in her face, in truth;
I introduced her to my friends
With light and careless bow; I gave
Her not a tear; and people said
"How she is brave!"

Now grief is come again, and she
Is purple-robed and awful-eyed.
Now all my friends are turned away
In loathing from my stricken side,
And laughter sickens on the lips
That played me false or did not know
They took the name of Grief in vain
A year ago!

When Sorrow Lifts My Latchstring

When sorrow lifts my latchstring,
May I go out with grace
And give the mournful stranger
A welcome to the place;

Put by her shawl and bonnet
And brew her fragrant tea,
And never let her sharp eye
Surprise a tear from me.

If I be bright and cheery,
If I be firm and strong,
Mayhap she'll not be staying
To try my courage long,

And though my heart be heavy
Where it was light before,
At least she shall not carry
Gossip from my door!

The Beauty Shop

I'd like to run a Beauty Shop.
I think it would be fun
To wash and starch a scowly face
And hang it in the sun;
To snip a dimple here and there,
Eliminate a pout,
Embroider in with twinkle-stitch
And press all wrinkles out.

I'd advertise a specialty
Of skilful nose-repair;
I'd fix high-bornful, scornful ones
And lead with tender care
The wandering and wayward ones
That poke about the place,
To home and duty; one apiece
On everybody's face.

For mouths that had been turning down
To grow the other way
I'd teach a round of little songs,
Ecstatically gay;
In short, the crabbiest customer
In just one hour with me,
Would permanently waive his gloom
And smile delightfully!

A Prayer For All The Time

Give me the heart that looks for lovely things
And lips that tell them in a hundred ways,
High faith and splendid courage, noble truth,
A kindly humor, a generous praise.
Oh, beautiful upon the mountain are
The feet of him that brings good tidings; Lord,
My little doling out of love and cheer
Is Thine abundant Word.
Let me not find delight in censuring;
Let me be kind, be large in charity,
And lofty-souled. Let small uncleannesses
And poisoned breaths go by unknown by me.
Let me not prostitute my own good brain
Devising mischief, nor, when Life is sweet,
Discover little hidden paths of pain
To unsuspecting feet.

Legacy

You shall have gilded summits and shining stairways
Where the others have only stormy sky:
You shall have faery blossom and leafy magic
The others will never see when they go by;
You shall have Spring-song in the snowy silences,
Consecration in lilies, comfort from rain,
And feet that follow with sad, unmistakable swiftness
After the joy that is closed to pain.

You shall have secret sobbing and hidden travail
Where others can lay them down and sleep;
You shall have starry vigil in lonely places
While they make merry who have not tryst to keep;
You shall have Lancelot's vision in perfect splendour
When the others will only stand and stare,
And oh, my heart, my heart, you will end in breaking
And the others – will not even care.

The Climber

I shall be always lonely.
Young trees grow high
That are forever searching
The sky.

But I would rather struggle
To watch clouds pass
Than clutter up a lifetime
With grass.

Affinity

As deep, slow chords of music stately sound
Like bells through all the temple of my soul,
And wake their yearnings to diviner things,
So between earth and that vast upturned bowl
Of heaven kindle longings and desires.
The mountain peaks are slender arms that rise
From flowing sleeves of lacy mists to make
Them shining contact with the blending skies.

Where rides the great ship slowly out to sea,
Somewhere upon the silver edge of space,
Before her ever and forever meet
Ocean and sky in unashamed embrace.
And now, when purple twilight falls around
The forest, on a darkly distant hill
Where waits one tense young poplar, suddenly
A watching star drops – hovers – and is still.

Closing Time

But yesterday I found a little shop
Set in a friendly, shabby thoroughfare,
Where an old man moved happily among
The lovely gewgaws he had gathered there;
Such delicate fine old lace in lengths
Jealously measured; teakwood boxes; strings
Of pale seed-pearls; a tinted satin fan;

Glass exquisitely spun and pewter things.
He fumbled here and there and touched each one
Contentedly in its accustomed place,
And I remember how the sun-gold made
A radiance upon his proud old face.

I hope that I, when I am growing old,
May have such lovely chattels of my own,
Frail, dusty dreams and exquisite old joys,
Spun crystal laughters I can tend alone;
White prayers stitched on shadowed tapestries
And shining carven faiths that cannot break –
And when the sun comes slanting to my door,
The last of day, I hope that it will make
A halo round my head, and I will stand
Upon the threshold counting happily
My own, that I have loved, in order there.
"Dear little shop, goodnight –"
                                          and turn the key.

God's Piper

Slight and shy and nondescript,
Down the April way he came,
Barefoot lad without a purse,
Beggar lad without a name.
Only as he moved, the leaves
Leaned to whisper love to him,
And the water-lilies yearned
From the silver river-rim
To his feet. Soft-breasted birds
Came and fluttered round his head,
And the light wind stirred his hair,
Laughing at the things he said.
If you asked him what he piped,
He would smile and answer you:
"Whatsoever things are pure,
Whatsoever things are true,
Like the hawthorn's veil of bloom,
Like the linnet on her nest,
Like a babe's uncovered eyes,

33

Least of things and loveliest."
Did he leave no shapely print
Of his young, glad, restless feet,
Did no echo follow him,
Fairy music, faint and sweet,
Does it matter, save that he
Passed, an eager spirit-boy,
In his ragged robe of dream,
Piping beauty, piping joy?

One Daffodil

One daffodil's a lovely thing –
I think there is too much of Spring,
We miss in glory so complete
How every little thing is sweet;
Too many flying ribbands where
The earth's white throat has been so bare
And, for the very moment after
Winter, too much soft bird-laughter.
When all the world's a loveliness,
What is one pretty more or less?

If April meant just this – that from
The broken flesh of earth, in some
Hushed, tender moment, should arise
Toward the sun, toward the skies,
One slim, green swaying body, grace
Personified, a piquant face
As golden as a star – ah me!
How we should look to 't tremblingly
If this were all there is of Spring!
One daffodil's a lovely thing...

The Uncomforted

I know. There will be other Springs,
And yet one only Spring for me,
When Love came trembling from my heart
Like blossom on the cherry-tree.

I know. The lark will still return
And lift his darling throat as then,
But never more for me will be
The first heart-shaking note again.

The Bird I Do Not Know

Long, long before the waiting hills have frocked themselves in green,
Before the earliest daffodils have spread their golden sheen,
While yet the woodland way I go is crisp beneath my feet,
I hear the Bird-I-Do-Not-Know call distantly and sweet.

Not all the forest harmonies that later flood the air
Nor all the blossom canopies that whiten everywhere
Will set my eager soul aglow with such fierce joy as when
The gypsy Bird-I-Do-Not-Know comes calling me again!

O follow by the finger of the silver little spring
And find the violets I love and miss no tender thing
Of all sweet things that rouse and start – but never seek to see
What faithful, little singing heart brings April back to me!

Prodigal

If life is a garden,
Then I shall bend low
To look for small laughters,
Stand on tiptoe
To reach me a branch of
The whitest white song,
Wrap me in a lilac mirth
As I dance along

If life is a garden,
Then I shall toss the red
Confetti of its petals
High over my head:
When the sap withers
In the stem of me
Time enough for pining
And for penury!

Horoscope

In ten or maybe twenty years
I shall have taught me not to weep,
And joy and sorrow, triumph, tears
Will lightlier lie on me than sleep.

For ten or twenty years, maybe,
I shall be dreadful wise; but then,
If the gods be middling kind with me,
I shall be able to weep again.

Walking

I know this is a strange, fantastic thought,
But I have been conjecturing today
How all the folk who ride in motor-cars
And look at me that lofty, absent way,
Will feed in Heaven Street; if they will crowd
Together, dumbly, like a flock of sheep,
And have forgotten how their limbs perform
And that exultant rhythm a heart can keep
That moves to weariness. Oh, will the air
Of Heaven be keen, the harps be loud, to shake
Them back to beauty? They have been asleep,
Or blind, or dull, or slaved; they could not take
Their spirits from a crowded road. They missed
An old man's fiddled tune, a lame girl's smile,
And how the lilacs smelled and how the rain
Blew softly silver every little while.
God might be standing in a cottage-door
Calling young children to Him happily,
God might be standing in a cottage-door,
Haloed and bright, and they would never see.

Maybe, though, I am wrong. Maybe, indeed,
It's hunting quiet Heaven Street they are,
The queer, grim, anxious folk who thunder by,
Lofty and absent, in a motor-car.

Storm

I have been watching how the sky all day
Has wrung unquiet hands in body-grief,
And I have wondered in my foolish way
What she was waiting for, for her relief.
Darkened with grey contortionings of cloud,
Since that first red, unhealthy flush of Dawn,
It seemed as if she agonized, sweat-browed,
Above the anxious world she leaned upon.
Sick sky! From pain to cataclysmic pain
She moves, and gives her body, and is torn,
Till, in a silver weltering of rain,
A thousand flowers waken and are born.

Beguiled

There was a grass-grown, rutted lane, and a grey bird in a tree
Crying "Come"; there were the venturesome, gypsy feet of me,
There was a gap in the battered fence where the wire had fallen low,
And a briar rose on a knoll ahead, and what could I do but go?
And when I was over the fence there was a crooked little way
Winding down and down. (Part of me whispered not to stay,
But the rest of me never listened!) There was a purple patch ahead,
And a frog came up and called to me out of his oozy bed.
The river had thrown a grist of pearl right to my very feet,
And there were bouquets of wild strawberries, scarlet and warm and sweet,
Fern in the rocks, and harebells, and a place for me to curl
In the deep, warm sand and stare at the silver fish in the sunlit swirl.
A turtle came out of deep water and walked with his queer pad-pad,
And nothing bothered or spoke to me. Everything seemed glad
To have me there; and I never knew, but now I'm telling you why,
If the bird in the grass-grown wheedles, whistle and swagger by:
Don't be coaxed! Part of me never stirred nor answered when
The rest of me said it was time to climb the broad highway again!

The Little Pale Prince

The little, pale Prince goes riding by,
And Derek and Nathan and I,

At the door of the shop and the gate of the field,
Stand watching him pass, and our lips are sealed
To silence. Into the light he goes,
And round his figure the dust clouds close.

Then Derek turns back to his little shop,
And silvery shavings drop
From his plane as he smooths at the shining board,
And Derek makes song for the Master Lord
Whose faithful 'prentice and slave is he –
Jesus, workman of Galilee!

And Nathan goes back to the good, grey earth,
And patiently tends at the birth
Of the little, green grain from the laboring sod,
And Nathan, who sweats for each torn, wet clod,
He whispers: "This is my pride to do,
The Lord God planted a garden too!"

And back to the tranquil hills I go
Where, drifting like the scattered snow,
Are the little, new lambs who wait my care,
The little, weak lambs like the one He bare
To safety, cherished against His breast,
And I tell myself: "Lad, thou art blest!"

The little, pale Prince goes riding by,
And there is a grief in his eye
For the bare, little shop and the field and the hill,
Or is it for us who are standing so still
And might be watching him wistfully,
Derek and Nathan and me?

Lad, If Thee Be Wavering

Lad, if thee be wavering
In they heart 'twixt these and me,
Hills aswoon with purple dream,
Leaf-love in a tree,
Fingers of the April moon
Twining softly through thy hair,

Tongues of little hidden streams
Whispering thee there,
Never doubt nor disobey,
Go and kneel at Beauty's shrine,
Then, if still thee be so sad
For my hand in thine,
Turn that dear, fair head and steal
Forth thy fingers happily:
Troth, is not thy little maid
Kneeling here by thee?

Bittersweet

I shall be alone, alone, alone,
For I will walk the hidden lofty Way
Of dreamers. I will breathe a sweetened air
And know the lyric things that skylarks say.
One song shall make me faint with loveliness,
One hyacinth my hungry spirit feed,
One leaning star shall bear me to the ground,
One wisp of childish laughter be my creed.
I hold the key to beauty and to truth,
Love blossoms crimson where I lay my hand,
I – I have lift the veil that covers God
And raptured cried, "I see. I understand."
My heart is but a magnet to His touch,
I know that I shall know, for I have known.
I am a poet. I will walk the Way,
But I shall go alone, alone, alone.

The Unfinished Prayer

She fell asleep before she said "Amen,"
For she had taken many steps that day
And labored with her hands and with her heart,
And now she was too tired, almost, to pray.
Not extraordinary her routine:
A home to keep, four hungry mouths to feed,
Four little bodies to be cleansed and clothed –
But oh, her work seemed never done! Indeed,

She went to bed sometimes on a regret,
Her sleep was often troubled with the thought
Of this and that small thing she had put off,
And this and that, alas, she had forgot!
She tried so hard to have a tranquil faith
But keeping brave and harder, keeping sweet,
Took so much heart that by the end of day
Her weariness was aching and complete.

She fell asleep before she said "Amen,"
Worn out with laughter and with love and care,
And God looked down upon her shadowed cheek
And smiled and stooped for her unfinished prayer,
And turned it gently over in his hand,
Eager and soft and so uncomforted:
"It has a broken wing, but none the less
Somehow it seemeth beautiful!" He said.

Such Lovely Things

I have seen such lovely things
As a low roof thatched with snow,
Powdered gold on grey moths' wings,
Young trees flushed with blossom-blow,
All these – and a clovered sea
With its swift, upsailing barque,
But the loveliest come to me
When the world is dark...

I have heard the poet-bird
Tell his raptures to the Dawn,
Boys' bell-voices I have heard
In a bright-toned carillon,
Violins in a symphony
And an ancient, praying mill,
But my own heart sings for me
When the world is still...

Pilgrimage

Pilgrimage is only sweet if you must say good-bye,
If there be tender little things to travel in your mind,

If every little house you pass and every garden cry
The little house and garden that you had to leave behind.

Pilgrimage is only sweet with half a heart to go,
And half a heart a-waiting for the other half's return,
If there be voices whispering how they will miss you so,
And little fires kept bright for you and little lamps that burn.

You may be off to London-Town to supper with the King,
Or just to Kew in blossom-time. I care not where nor when,
Pilgrimage is only sweet with your remembering
The path that led your feet away will bring them home again.

September

I like the world untidy as it is today
Dandelions all gone mad and danced away,
Slattern geese trolloping a lazy trail,
Golden-rod rusting on a clean fence rail,
Beads of scarlet berries strung on any breeze,
Bits of broken sunsets falling through the trees!

The Pastoral Visit to the Poorhouse

Laws, I ain't complainin'! 'Course if it's true, it's true,
Only I won't feel right at home, spangled and starched and new,
Up in the proper Heaven, he's bound to take me to!

Mebbe I shouldn't speak so, but it seems I couldn't bear
(After my own old make-shift clothes I been so used to wear)
Struttin' 'round in a grand, white gown, with a crown upon my hair.
Ever'thing else I'll come to like, I guess, though it will be queer
Playin' harps, after I've scrubbed the floor and washed down here,
Laws! But I dread them brand-new robes with a kind o' sinkin' fear!

Think I'll ask, when he comes again, if up in his Heaven, p'raps,
After angels' robes is sewn and the bits fall from their laps,
Couldn't I make me a nice, neat dress and an apern from the scraps?

Spinster

In all her soul's drab merchandise
Miss Hester had three lovely things:
A fragile, scented memory,
A hope with eager, shining wings,
A little wistful, timid dream.
One morning, curiously gay,
She moved her other wares and set
The three bright treasures on display.
Nobody saw Miss Hester crouch
Behind her soul's grey-curtained glass,
Or knew she hushed her heart to hear
The praise of people who should pass.
They saw her memory, and laughed;
They found her hope and stared surprise –
Miss Hester snatched her dream away,
The shamed tears crowding to her eyes.
Of doubt and such dark merchandise
Miss Hester keeps an ample store;
Once she had lovely things to sell,
But no one wants them anymore.

Prayer Against Fame

God, whatever else you give me,
Never give me fame,
Let no stranger tongue manhandle
My own father's name.
Let me walk and sing and worship
To Your eyes alone,
Not that gait and song and prayer
Will be told and known.
Give me windswept ways to wander,
Lonely ways and sweet,
Rather than the restless people
Scabbing at my feet,
God, and put me in a dungeon
With my misery,
Rather than a cage, with faces
Staring in at me!

The Flighty Commodity

I envy all these tranquil folk
Whom Heaven weighs so carefully.
They never either bump the earth,
Or ride the scales sky-high, like me.
I think it must be fine to sit,
With lofty smile and cautious eye,
And measure equal parts of joy
And gloom to every passerby.
This hectic life I have to live,
One moment burdened down with woe,
The next in soaring ecstasy,
It's very hard on me, you know,
My breathing's always disarranged
With rapid journeys through the air;
My face unfolds and blows about,
My heart is simply everywhere!
Still, every cloud is sliver-lined,
Some day I'll bounce up on a shelf
And stay there, reaching down to you
With joyful parcels of myself!

Noel

O Little Christ! O little Christ!
Well may Thy wondering baby eyes
Look on us with a grave surprise
Who keep tonight the simple tryst.

Not shepherds we in homely shrift,
Forsaking fen and field and fold,
To stumble o'er the starry wold
And bring some foolish, lovely gift.

We be indeed a motely throng,
On shabby feet, in shining cars,
Yet looking to the selfsame stars,
And thrilling to the old, old song.

The sinner and the saint draw near:
Who doubts, who stands by sophistry,

Who points the manger avidly,
The children of the day are here.

O little Christ, despise us not,
Nor see our eyes with fear bemused,
Nor hear our speech with prides confused,
Nor penetrate our puny thought;

Let but the wise man come tonight
And shamefully admit him fool.
Let the self-righteous flee his rule
And plead him sinner in Thy sight.

Remember not our pride of years,
Nor yet our arrogance of youth,
Give us to bear the gift of truth
And tell our helplessness, our fears,

Our yearning toward the simple tryst
In all the troubled maze of things,
The Song of Songs that swells and sings
Thy happy birth, O little Christ!

The Grateful Guest

I must be very careful when
At last I go away
To leave this earthly chamber just
As pretty and as gay
As when I crossed its threshold. He
Who brought me here a guest,
He has been gentle to my needs
And made my sojourn blest.
He gave me day and eager feet
And dusk and sweet content,
And laughter was a creed for me
And love a sacrament.
Now let me leave no crumpled faiths
About, no dingy fears,
Let there be no long sighs for me,
No wondering, no tears,
But simply here a book that falls

Wide-open to a prayer,
And reddened embers on the hearth,
And fragrance in the air
Of my bright words. And if I leave
Behind me any thing,
Let it be very beautiful
For my remembering.

Sabbath

I like this day that God has planned,
The valley village, still and sweet,
Within its cup of sun, and spanned
In cloudless blue, long shadows meet
Reposefully of old, old trees
In friendly conclave on the snow,
And little, blurry shadows tease
Among them, dancing as they go
Each little house is shut away
Alone with its peculiar cares,
This is the holy Sabbath day,
And let him mar its peace who dares!
The very smoke curls tranquilly
From cottage roofs and in the sun
Sedate old dogs with dignity
Prepare their slumbers, one by one.
At length, from some far watching hill
The church-spire cries its carillon,
And, though the streets are gentle still,
The languor suddenly is gone.
Each little house its door flings wide
And forth, arrayed in careful best,
The father, with a sober pride,
Ushers his own and loveliest.
Obedient to some wondrous thing,
Some age-old, sweet, compelling Strength
That brought their fathers comforting
And safely harbored them at length,
From every way they come till I
Imagine Fingers wide outspread

To gather all these treasures nigh,
And keep them safe and comforted

O wise and happy souls who own
This pristine Sabbath! We have strayed
Who other Sabbath days have known –
This is the Day the Lord hath made.

The Fiddler in Church

I saw last Sunday in a little church,
(A white and lowly, but a gentle place).
In one shy corner near the organ-loft,
An old, old man with such a happy face,
Fiddling the hymns out with an earnest bow.
His music, high and thin and subtly sweet,
Ran like a silver hem along the grave,
Grey tapestry of singing, making neat
True knots of melody to end each verse.
The fiddler's eyes but rarely left the score,
They seemed to love the dear, familiar thing
That had been comfort oftentimes before.
I liked to think that God was listening
From His high Heaven for the fiddle-strain,
One Hand upraised to hush the golden harps,
That this wee, gallant voice might sound more plain;
I liked to think of angels making room
In that devout, celestial symphony,
For one old fiddler, when his moment came
To join the players. Oh, it seemed to me
So cheering and so beautiful a thing
That he, with care and labor in his wake,
Should be thus tranquil to his summoning,
To sit and smile, and with his fiddle make
Him little hymns, old, dear, familiar tunes,
No troubled, complex thing folk could not know,
But simply, "I believe" – a good old man
Telling his faith out with his fiddle-bow.

The Church of The Holy Trinity, Toronto, Canada

I think our Lord, were he to come on earth
And choose with His own eyes a dwelling place,
Would have it not too big and not too grand,
But grey and kindly, sweetened with the grace
Of all old things.
I think that He would like

No garish splendor and no gross display;
A house that held a tenderness for all
Who hungered and who happened by that way;
A house whose door was open to the street,
A house whose roof looked upward to the sky,
Whose windows set a light of comforting
Upon their sills, for strangers passing by.

How rich a hospitality this house
Would have – the filling Bread, the living Wine,
The lavish Hand to give, the listening Ear,
The Heart o'erflowing with a Love Divine.
I think our Lord, were He to happen on
So sweet a place, would smile, and whisper then,
"Blest be this little House, and Heaven be here
To all who come a-seeking it. Amen!"

Faux Pas

I wish you had not come so eagerly
With votive friendship. When I saw you first
All things about you interested me.
I wanted then to learn your best and worst
In slow, delighting phases; for I knew
That something you had hidden, rich and fine,
Within the casual and smiling you
Might mate with something beautiful of mine.
I wish you had been silent or been slow
To speak, and had withheld the lovely thing
I wanted. Now I shall not prize it so.
I should have liked to watch its beckoning
A little while, and dream and pray and walk

Up softly then and touch it at my will.
Alas! Why must you lean and wave and knock
The white, young taper from your window-sill?

The Organ Recital

Go tell the Master of this holy House,
Since He hath entertained me in this wise,
There is not any vow I will not take
To serve Him as is fittest in His eyes.

Tell Him that I am waiting in the dim
And lovely shadows of His dwelling-place
To hear His will: my hand and heart are His
When the high summons comes to do His grace.

I will be shining knight to seek His Grail,
Or meek nun cloistered in His anchorhold,
I will be good physician for His sick,
String to His harp or shepherd to His fold.

I will break bread to feed His hungry mouths,
As He hath broken to my spirit here,
Or keep sweet comfort for His weary feet,
As mine have found this sanctuary dear.

Now, with His silence and His sunset round,
A willing vassal waits upon her knees,
Her soul one ache of listening – Ah, go,
Go tell mine Host that I am ready, please.

If I Have To Be A Little Old Lady

If I have to be a little old lady,
The kind of old lady I'll have to be
Is wrinkled and rosy and tender and cosy,
A sort of nicer edition of me.

I'll want to run a little shop where
Folk can come and carry away
Comforts, all sizes. (The pleasant surprise is
Nobody ever requested to pay.)

Loaves of comfort for hungry mouths and
Comforty blankets for shabby feet,
Comfort flowers for dreary hours,
Babykin comforters, fat and sweet.

I'll have to be dressed in a clean, white pinny,
The sort of pinny that smells of sun,
And customers choosey or very refusey,
I'll open my arms out and love each one.

I'm quite aware that it sounds so silly,
But nevertheless, as I say to me,
If I have to be a little old lady,
That's the old lady I'll have to be!

To a Despoiler

This is all of Life to me: this thing
You hold as valueless. Right from my baby days
I quested for it, thought the capering
Of sun-motes hid it; sought it in childish ways
To wrest it from a butterfly, a bee;
Hurt myself, cried, and started out again.
All through the years it danced ahead of me
And I eluded signs and shouts and men
To find it.

(Bows on fiddle-throats can show
The pale, ecstatic scar; an iris-breath
Is hot with it; the first glad, frightened glow
Of Dawn; the last sharp, tuneful sigh of Death.)

I sang. And suddenly, from out of the vain
And ghostly shadows it was sweetly mine,
All its brave heritage of dream and pain
Warming my spirit like a god's own wine.

And you are pouring, drop by precious drop,
The draught upon the ground, and wiping dry
The cup that held it. Will you see, and stop,
Or will you squeeze the vessel out till I
Rock in white anguish?

Even then, when you
Lay the old chalice from your selfish hand,
Broken, that might have been a Grail – who knew?-
Will you be sorry? Will you understand?

The Leaner

All her soft life she has had someone's arm
To lean upon. Her feet have never grown
Accustomed to their burden. (Can you harm
A limp-winged butterfly, or leave alone
A bird that will not fly from horses' hooves?)
She has been sadly safe from wind and rain.
Padding along in comfortable grooves
Of care and kindness. Kept apart from pain,
She learned no splendid lessons of her sins.
She had no will to sing and dare and do,
She made her life in lace, with trembling pins.

Strange to be wondering, when she is dead,
How she has fared, who had no single thing
For Heaven to see.
Think you some angel said:
"Forgive her, God. She hath a drooping wing ..."?

Night-Content

Just to be tired is beautiful
Is it not meet that I,
When petals fold and birds fly home,
And long grey shadows lie
Across the tranquil breast of earth,
Should feel a deep content
Of weariness upon my limbs?
I too my strength have spent
In splendid ways; I too shall drink
This matchless draught that brings
Return of joy for all the day's
High-hearted journeyings!

Hushed wing, spent rose and waiting star,
And ah, but Night is sweet
To us who walk the crowded ways
With such exultant feet!

Creed

I climb a little stair
From day to day
That leads I know not where;
Indeed, I do not care,
So that young children play
From flight to shining flight
And laugh and sing,
And tiredly bring at night
Each one his little light
To guide his journeying
Up, up, where through the deep
Meadows of stars,
Cropping a sky of sleep,
White angel lambkins leap
At golden pasture-bars;
Up, up, where like a bell
In the lost skies,
Tenderly, I can tell,
Some Voice that loves them well
Makes babes their lullabies.

Prologue

When she was Anne-a-little-girl
She clapped her hands at everything:
A drop of water was her pearl,
A circle was her fairy-ring,
And not a day and not a night
But brought its moment of delight!

Then she grew analytical
And knew her how and why and what,
And oh, so fluently could tell

Were this a pretty lie or not;
And growing suddenly so wise,
She lost the wonder from her eyes:

Until at last, one burdened day,
She chanced upon the sorry truth
That analyzing joys away
Is quite a silly game. Forsooth,
She wisely takes her joys since then
As Anne-a-little-girl again!

A Little Boy's Valentine to His Mother

Dear little Knight, thou must not know
Thy Lady loved this missive so;
Surely a lady is but wise
Who tells not all things in her eyes.
Therefore, I took with gentle grace
The scarlet token edged with lace
Thou brought'st with such darling air
Of dignity, and made with care
My tender, grave acknowledgement.
With that, dear Knight, thou'lt be content,
Nor know at dark thy Lady came
This couch unto, and spoke thy name
And softly smiled and softly wept
And kissed her lover while he slept.

Defendant

Someday I too may choose to be
Among the greybeard company
That hug this fireside, making sage
Converse on the decadent age
And delving in the dusky lore
Of all good ages gone before,

But not today. Today the street
Is gay with marching crocus feet,
And minstrel robins swagger by

On winds that strum a viol sky,
This April wags a silver tongue
And, good your worships – I am young!

A Little Girl Looks at a Sampler

I like you for your woolly tree
With leaves sewn in so carefully,
That blossom in your garden-bed:
I like you for the woolly seat
Where, shaded from the summer heat,
A quaint and woolly courting pair
Look out at me and do not care:
I like you for your pretty frame
And someone's shy, old-fashioned name
Down in this corner, and the year
In woolly figures, bold and clear.

But oh, I love you for the way
A little ghost-girl, sweet and gray,
Sits stitching at you every day.

The Starvelings

God's is the Hand that feeds this hungry flock
That chirp and crowd and pluck His garment's hem,
Or, if there be two bolder than the rest
That climb His shoulder, why, he suffers them
And doles out His crumbs impartially – such sweet
White crumbs as sunsets or a rose-pot hung
With moon-vine, or the little lyres of throats
That babies thumb with laughter, or a tongue
Of poppy-flame upon a charred black sod,
Or slim rain-fingers bright with rainbow rings,
Or falling stars, or, from the ferny copse,
The lovely startled rush of hern-wives' wings.
God's is the Hand that strews thus lavishly
These mystic fragments of the bread that feeds
And breeds new chafing hunger until life
Itself is swallowed in the soul's vast needs.

Some little pulsing tribute of a song
We pay Him, and we snatch the shining fare,
And patiently He multiplies His loaves
And throws each soul what beauty it can bear.

May Rain

I think it pattered happily
On grey-thatched rooves of cloud, and ran
In crystal globules down the sky,
Before the joyous day began.

I think it fell to earth like some
Green-tendrilled, silver-budding vine,
And every star leaned forth to see
Her image in the passing shine.

I think it brushed the breasts of birds,
And gathered merry liquid notes
To make dainty chorus for
A thousand lyric raindrop throats

And then I think the apple-bloom
Poured down in jealous petal-showers,
For all the lovely May is drowned
In sweet of rain and scent of flowers.

The Lilac tree

She is very old
And grey and bent,
And for months and months
She is well content
To huddle down
By the orchard wall
And doze and dream
Of nothing at all.

Only in May
She calls for her
Wedding satin
And lavender,

And opens the gate
And walks in Spring,
Remembering
And Remembering...

Apple – Blossoms

Who decorated the apple-tree
With little pink roses?
I asked of the breeze who it could be,
And the breeze supposes
The sun and the rain. I asked them. They
Put their heads together
And whispered softly, "It was May
With her tender weather."
May denies it, saucily cries,
"Now, little Miss Nancy,
Look at the leaves. Just use your eyes!
The leaves are dancey!"
Could they have waked in my sleep and hid
Their capers under
The dark? Who prettied my tree? Who did?
Who did, I wonder?
I'd like to be certain, especially
As a vain little bird plumps his feathers at me
And insists it was he.
Oh, who decorated my apple-tree?

Earth-Born

No eagle I to dare the splendid sun
With flaunting wings; no nightingale to breast
The winds of Dawn; I but the little one
Among God's birds, content to make my nest
In earth's grey tender fingers, walled about
With meadow-grass and shadow, with a sword
Of wind-blown iris staunchly barring out
Too friendly beasts.

Here, jealous of my hoard
Of happiness, I hide and have my dear,

And proudly housed, our babies. Here the dew
Marries the sweet red clover-bloom; and here
The fireflies dip their mystic flames in blue
Smooth dusk, and rise and shine and never tell
How just to climb the blackthorn fence and trace
The bindweed trail and see a tall harebell
Nuzzling a rock, would find my hiding-place.
I, with one nest's simplicity of pain,
I am the least and blest of all God's birds,
And when the sky is silver-low with rain
I tell Him so in little silver words.

Refugee

I will go up to the woods again
And let me in through the vaulted door
To the sunlit nave, and then
Nothing will matter any more.

Here is a passive priestess done
With love and laughter and strife and stir,
She kindles her candles one by one
And does not dwell on the things that were:

Walling her spirit with sky and earth,
She does her penance to stones and trees,
She sweeps the floor with a holy mirth
And joins in the birds' bright liturgies:

But if ever a footfall wake the calm
Till the tall ferns tremble and draw apart,
She will snuff the taper and still the psalm
And bar the door with a beating heart.

I Met Some Little People

I met some Little People on a May-Day morning,
Coming out of Goodness-Knows and going on to Where,
For Dumple said a lily-pad and Dapple said a Rainbow,
And Dimple said for mercy's sake she really didn't care!

Dumple was the roundest one and had to walk the slowest,
So Dumple came ahead and puffed a little pipe of clay,
And tiny rings of fairy-smoke came rolling down the meadow,
And yellow flames of dandelions lit themselves that day.

Dapple was the shining one and swung a dewdrop lanthorn
Wherever there were lazy little sleepers in their beds,
And that was when the butterflies shook out their jewelled sashes
And rose in golden companies above our startled heads.

But Dimple was the little one and Dimple had a basket,
And Dimple plied her needle when she thought I didn't see,
And that was how the crimson buds in crooked rows came straggling,
Sweet and small and knotted, on the crab-apple tree!

The Empty Little House

Nobody ever stops to see
What flowers grow in there,
Nor if the lilac tree is out,
Nor what the windows wear.
And oh, the little house must look
As if it didn't care!

No fingers ever lift the latch
Of such a rusty gate,
Nor footsteps hurry up the path,
Afraid they might be late.
And oh, the little house must act
As if it didn't wait!

And when prospective buyers come
And poke about and peer,
And cry their caustic comment on
The hallowed things and dear,
The broken little house must smile
As if it didn't hear!

The Toys That Are Left Out Nights

If ever I go travelling after tea,
The very most sorrowful sight I see
Is a Cart left out on a lonely lawn,
Or a little Toy Dog with his master gone;
Or (this is the dreadfullest thing of all)
The front door shut on a sobbing Doll.

The hundreds of tiny tears I've dried
For woebegone Toys that were left outside,
The stories I've told and the songs I've sung,
The motherless Dollie's clothes I've hung
On the rose-bush peg, and the care I've taken
Lest any I've got to sleep should waken!

And I tell you this, little girls and boys,
Who go to bed and forget your Toys:
Some night I'll travel about the town,
Picking up Toys that were just thrown down,
The Dogs, the Dollies, and all the others,
And find them brand-new fathers and mothers.

Encounter in Vagabondia

As I came up the Highway,
(And it was early June
And all the world a-sparkling)
I met a poor gossoon
Who could not see the sunshine
For staring through a frown,
And he told me he was tired out
Looking for a town.

Then oh, the merry morning
Flung down its laughter red,
And mirth swept through the meadow
And rocked each cloverhead;
A bluejay screamed derision,
A squirrel chattered scorn,
A bullfrog from a brook's edge
Blew a taunting horn!

I had no words to tell him
(The road was wide and sweet
And hung with dewdrop lanterns)
Where he should find a street;
I had no will to wise him
(The road was green and bare),
The folks in dingy houses
Smothered over there.

And when I tried to point him
A milestone and a name,
The bright winds held my heartstrings,
The young larks sang my shame;
And I got up and left him
A-staring up and down,
(The Lord forgive the numbskull!)
Looking for a town.

Insignia

She asked no station by His side
When He was glorified of men
Who saw His miracles; she claimed
No credit then

Only, when that dark ocean of
His insult swept away the other,
Proudly she stood beside the Cross,
His Mother.

Wings

I think of Summer as sweet with wings
For myriad journeyings.
June or sooner they all unfold,
Wings of silver and wings of gold,
Wings of velvet and wings of silk,
Black as sable and white as milk,
Flecked with scarlet and fringed with green,
Opalescent and phosphorine,
Slowly flutter and swiftly rise
Over the blossoms, into the skies!

Nothing matters except to be
Flaunting eager and jaunting free:
Lightly rock on a petal-rest,
Softly dip to a cloud's grey breast;
Dream, but never lie down to sleep,
Many are breathless trysts to keep;
Own no boundaries, see no bars,
Here are lilies – but there are stars!
You birds, you butterflies, all God's things
That travel on wings – on wings!

Benny-Boy's Feet

When Benny-Boy goes down the street,
Straight ahead point both his feet,
Each one eager to be knowing
Just where Benny-Boy is going

When Benny-Boy comes home again,
Right Foot leans to Left Foot, then
Dreadful' tired (smiles Benny's mother)
And dreadful' glad to have each other!

Twilight Pool

By Twilight Pool the long elms lean
On gnarled elbows, lost in thought.
Young birches, garlanded in green,
Their lovers' silver screeds have brought
To dream upon; and round the brink
Sweet iris-children in the care
Of nursemaid winds, come down to drink
And see their pretty faces there.

For me by lonely Twilight Pool
The sky makes stars on dusky wings,
The maid-moon from her three-cloud stool
Lets down her golden hair and sings;
And saddened waters break their veil,
Elaine's white hands to anguish through,
And phantom barges stately sail
Without the aid of wind or crew.

No lad by lovely Twilight Pool
Shall hold my hand and walk with me
Unless the maid-moon lift her rule
And sing him love and witchery;
Unless the ghost-prow, pale and dim,
Make all his senses die and start,
And winged stars fly down to him
And silence crowd against his heart.

Windflower

O shy white virgin of a flower,
I know the beauty of your hour

Who love your love for his unrest
And lightly lean upon his breast
And dusk and dawn abandon there
Your fragrant kisses in his hair:

Whose frail young body reaches up
To bear its consecrated cup
For moth and sun and wren and bee
To kindle in its ecstasy.

And yet who sets her trembling feet
In lonely little ways and sweet,
Lest anything but God should trace
Her passion to its hiding-place.

O little flower, content to go
"Whichever way the wind doth blow"!

The Spying Townley House

The Townley house on Teller Street is shiny-red and new,
I s'pose that now it's built itself it's nothing else to do
But keep a watch on little boys when they are walking by,
But my, I hate that Townley house for being such a spy!

It's put itself as close upon the street as it can get,
With porches and verandahs that are closer even yet,
And every window has a lamp for fear it couldn't see
Exactly what was happening to little boys like me!

If I forget my grammar 'course the Townley house it hears,
It's got such great big flapping green-and-white-striped awning ears,
It peeps behind its pillars, and it laughs behind its hand,
It's shockingly bad-mannered, though it thinks itself so grand!

And nights when I'm at homework if I hear the doorbell ring,
I wouldn't be surprised if Mama jumped like anything
To find the Townley house had come from Teller Street to say
"Your little boy forgot to lift his cap to me today!"

The Old Gardener

Strange how Danny's flowers know
This is Danny – shuffling so.

Yet the young green grasses lie
Quiet when he stumbles by,
And the proud rose lays her hold
On his coat-sleeve, worn and old.

Once the greedy larkspur drew
From his eyes their youthful blue;
Once the poppies' splendid length
Fed upon his straight limbs' strength.

With his shrunken shadow pressed
Pitifully to her breast,
Now the grey dial tells the sun:
"Danny's hour is almost done."

Still his anxious birds fly near,
Pleading, "Master, Heaven is here!"

The Vain Delphinium

First she told us excitedly,
"I'm glad I'm pretty.
I'm glad I'm me!"

Then she chuckled, "Oh my, good people,
I'm glad I'm tall. I
Can see a steeple!"

Now she's bragging, "I'm glad I'm blue,
For so is the sky
I'm coming to!"

The Vegetable Man

When I'm a little bigger I am planning, if I can,
To drive a spottled wagon like the Vegetable Man.
I won't sell beets nor cabbages nor radishes 'cause they
Are lovely deep red spottles that I wouldn't give away;
I won't sell any onions, 'cause on sunny days they shine,
And shiny silver spottles are a favourite of mine;
And if you want potatoes I'm afraid I'd likely frown,
I wouldn't want to touch the spottles done in dusty brown.
The butter beans? No, Madam. Every Tuesday you've been told
They're not for sale – my pretty finger-spottles made of gold!
I won't be selling lettuce. 'cause I have to have the green
To make the other spottles for the spaces in between;
But folk in bare grey houses will be watching at the door,
And folk who have been gloomy won't be gloomy anymore,
And folk who never laugh will laugh when down the dusty road
My lovely spottled waggon brings its vegetable load.

Nothing is Wiser Than Tall Trees

Nothing is wiser than tall trees
And nothing is as still;
Though winds lay fingers on their throats,
They only speak at will.
And yet tall trees are first to hear
The whispered summons of the Dawn,
And first of all the world to draw
Day's shining garments on.

For tall trees' fingers rain has gifts
Of opals set in silver rings,
Night wreathes star-daisies in their hair
And April brings them wings.
Or, borne on dusk, tall trees have felt
Diane's witch-horn arouse their breasts

And given their gallant shoulders for
The white moon's stirrup-rests.
All this to tell; and nothing told,
Save when my shy prayers rise,
And tall trees, watching through the night,
Speed them with quiet eyes.

Strange Beauty

There are the flowers of the sky
That only loose their petals when
The dusk goes softly hurrying by,
Or softly hurrying by again.

There is the perfume of the moon,
Witch-brew of ghostly flower-vagrants,
That leaves the very air aswoon
With sad and eerie silver fragrance.

And just at gloaming there are wings,
And murmurings, and deep thoughts swelling
In my heart of tender things,
Tender things – and not for telling.

A Forest Roof in Autumn

A forest roof in autumn is as softly thought a thing
As any Turkish prayer-rug in bronzy coloring
With stains of red and green.
And yet young angel boys who lean
From Heaven's windows, peering through the sun's transparent screen,
Must look with wistful eyes upon this earth-street far below,
Where bluebirds dip and scatter and the glad winds come and go,
And clouds in warm grey spirals make them whimsy traceries,
Where God has built His bonfires from a forestful of trees.

Apple-Song

Of all the pretty things
Ready for singing,

Gay, rosy, witty things
Swaying and swinging,
You can't do very wrong,
Singing an apple-song!

Sing of the baby buds
Making red kisses
In a May morning,
(A pretty song this is!)
Sing then of brown lads,
Slim lads and lasses,
Throwing green balls through
The orchard-grasses.
Sing of the dusty old
Woman-trees,
Apron-laps sagging
Down to their knees.
Sing a warm kitchen
With somebody there,
And apple-scent spicily
Sweet in the air.
Sing the red cheeks of
Apples that glow
Round the hearth-flame
In a worldful of snow.
Sing slumber songs for a
Sleeping old tree,
Heavy with dreams of the
April to be.

Sing rather softly,
But sweetly and happily,
Anything fragrant,
Leaf-and-sun dappley,
Anything orchard-born,
Anything appley!

The Scarecrow

Heigho and welladay!
Merry only comes to sad.

Walking down a greening way,
I have seen the only lad
I could lose my heart to, leant
Rakishly upon a stile,
There stood I and well-content
Not to look another mile!

Battered might his hat sit
Low upon his whimsy brow,
Yet he tipped the brim of it
In a pretty, swagger bow;
Tattered hung his coat-sleeve,
Yet he flung a crooked arm
Wide, as if to make-believe
He were owner of the farm!
Blushing, gaily did I go,
'Cross his field of golden grain,
With a foolish step and slow
Came I to the road again:
And they ask and I say "Nay,"
For a sorry dream I had,
Heighho and welladay –
But he was the darling lad!

An Old Body's Prayer

Oh Lord, I'm almost afraid to see
The things that's happening
All 'round me.
I want to ask You to think before
You tell the secret of
Any more.
Even if radio reach the sun,
You keep Your station a
Silent one
And steel bird-bodies fly high and far,
Oh, don't let anyone
Find a star!
I couldn't a-bear to poke and peer
And know the moment that
April's here;

I'm not for seeing myself clear through;
There's things I'm willing to
Leave to You.
I pray for the good of the human race –
But, Lord, You stay in Your
Rightful place!

Indian Summer

Summer is coming home again over the lang'rous hills
Up through the aisles of harvest-gold, under the orchard trees,
The dust of the rich year whites her brow, the earth's ripe crimson spills
Out of her arms, and the purple blood of the wild grape stains her knees.
Heavy her eyes with slumb'rous peace, drowsy with stilled desire,
High, sweet ways she has journeyed over since in the Dawn she went
Forth on her gay young pilgrimage; dew and gloaming and fire
Of the last red sunglow, each has given her splendid sacrament.

The young green April world and she grown goldenly grey together,
And all the gifts of the earth garnered under a smiling sky,
Now, old and tranquil and beauty-burdened, all in the winey weather,
Summer is coming home again over the hills to die.

The Road-Mender to Heaven

'I wouldn't be an Emperor, I wouldn't be a King,
I wouldn't change the job I have for gold or anything,
And yet from early morning till the sleepy sun goes down,
I only tend the little road that leads to Heaven-Town.

I help to keep it shining and I help to keep it sweet,
I brush away the dusty sins that clutter round my feet,
I send out birds of laughter and they fill the morning skies,
I bind up wings of damaged dreams like broken butterflies;
I plant a seed of kindness, then I wait behind a tree,
And pretty soon a friendship-flower grows and blooms for me;
I dig out little falsehoods and I throw them in a heap
And have a splendid bonfire, then I try to watch and keep
The worn-down places in the road all neatly patched with some
Good brand of faith, and when with harp and psalm the pilgrims come,
They ask me: "Little brother, we be weary with our sin.

O tell us, does the Warder wait to let a traveller in
Who longs for Heaven-comfort?" And I point them straight ahead.
"No heart goes up to Heaven-Town and is not comforted,"
I answer. And they ride away, and softly through the night
The friendly lamps of Heaven-Town are guiding them aright.

Then give to Kings and Emperors their crowns – I envy none
When Master comes to praise me for the bit of work I've done;
I dare not raise my eyes, but I be proud to hear Him say,
"God bless thee, little brother, for a spotless road this day!'"

Millionaire

The sorriest little boy I know
Is seventy years and nearly nine,
And hasn't as much of joy to show
As half of seventy – which is mine.
He sits all day with his face screwed up,
Counting the pennies he saved last year,
With two fists guarding his money-cup
From curious children playing near.
His body is withered for hide-and-seek,
His whistle is rusty for "Uncle Ned,"
He wants good wind on his warped head;
But nobody dares disturb his play
Save old Nurse Death for her sleepy boy,
Who'll trick and wheedle his feet away –
When other children may have his toy!

The Last Worshipper

And thus the cycle of the year
Turns slowly round to Autumn. Then
Do hill and vale and marsh and mere
Unite to bloom to God again.
White May was all too delicate,
And summer walked with careless feet,
But lo, this worshipper come late,
How she is passionate and sweet!
With swinging braids of sun-bright hair
And joyous, grave Madonnaed eyes,

Her passing is a breathless prayer,
Her step makes music down the skies,
And all earth's tired pulses stir
To last and lovelier effort: now
The fields are all gone gold for her,
And amethystine grapes her brow
Deep jewel; now a silken veil
Of such webbed silver that a star
May pierce its dimness, knows how pale,
Yet Juno-curved, her shoulders are.
Now amber-breasted birds or blue,
And butterflies with topaz wings,
Their gaudy patterns stencil through
On jade to mark her journeyings:
And scarcely has the round moon done
(The rose of worship in her blood)
Than quaffs the bronzed Indian sun
Her rapture in a ruby flood:
And as the vestal maid goes past,
Young maples hear her holy lyre,
And purge themselves of green and cast
Bright bodies on her altar-fire.

Oh earth, thine orisons are said,
And I have seen thee make the sign,
Thy last of flowering broke Him bread,
Thy final fruiting poured Him wine.

Books

Tonight in this warm, lamplit room,
I was the lady at her loom,
Dreaming of Camelot. And I
Was Cleopatra with a sigh
For my king-lover. I did tell
Most anguished beads for Gabriel.
I was that gypsy maid who drew
A heart's-blood patteran, straight and true!

While you, across the hearth, have fought
Such splendid battles; staked the spot

Where in a royal name you claimed
New lands; with Launcelot's ardour flamed
To knighthood vows; slain mighty foes;
Kept that white guerdon of a rose
Your lady gave; and made a song
Ten thousand years will bear along;
Even, perhaps, have wept and worn
A strange rough crown of plaited thorn!

Now, with the old, old sweet surprise,
We lift each other startled eyes
And smile to find us safe and near –
A happy ending, oh my dear!

The Shepherd Boy

He knelt beneath the starry skies
With that bright Vision in his eyes,
Too wonder-struck to move or rise.

They tapped his shoulder, rough but kind.
"We go, and do thou stay behind,
The ewes and little lambs to mind."

Was ever night so strange to see,
When hill and rock and leaf and tree
Stood forth in starlight brilliantly?

The grey sheep huddled close with fear,
And crept the crouching shepherd near,
His word of comforting to hear.
And soft he spoke and overawed,
Naming them gently with his rod,
"Born is the little Lamb of God."

Song

And if they ask I'll answer them with laughter,
And they'll be baffled then and turn away,
But I'll be busy for a long hour after
With all the shining things I could not say.

I'll have your eyes upturned in breathless wonder
To some grave star hung pendant in my sky,
While they, like troubled moths, go blindly under
The very lamps of God that light them by;

I'll feel your body throbbing to the largo
Of Dawn that beats slow beauty in my brain,
And watch your spirit bending to its cargo
Of sunset grief and loneliness and pain:

Wherever bud burns red or leaf turns falling,
Or frail snow frets the frosty wind at will,
I'll hear your rapturous calling, calling, calling,
And send my joyful halloo down the hill;

And they'll be starved for bread of our light breaking,
And golden apples of Hesperides
That in the moon of harvest you'll be shaking
From all our faery trees.

Blue Dusk

Blue fold on fold, the drowsy dusk descends upon the snow,
Blue wing on wing, the shadows close about the afterglow,
And rich blue wraiths of lovely things are drifting to and fro.

Gentian, delphinium, Canterbury bells,
Dewy-eyed forget-me-nots by moss-grey wells,
Marble of old terraces and mauve pearl shells.

Dull blue Wedgewood and Delft blue glossed,
Blue silk crinolines with sprigs embossed,
Pressed sweet lavender of old loves lost

Ice-blue sapphires in a silver frame,
Dark shrines jewelled with their candle-flame,
Drowned blue moonlight for the sea to claim.

Night's a frosted goblet with a brew of purple heather,
Blue grape, pomegranate, crushed down together,
And stars stirred in with a peacock's feather.

And blue on blue, blue fold on blue, the dusk creeps round my door,
Grown rich with all the fragrance of old dusks that bloomed before,
And never, once the stars come out, to blossom any more.

Understudy

I in a pool of candlelight,
God by His stars at night
Or in the golden flame of noon,
Or bowed by His grave moon,
Make poems out of shining things,
Deep water, wet leaves, wings.

All of God's things are mine to use,
The tender purple bruise
A hill makes, leaning on the sky,
The dark owl's stricken cry
And all the foolish brittle pain
Of crickets wanting rain.

But He with shadow, scent and vine
Shames any work of mine;
His frond of fern is mystery
So terrible to me
I tremble, being deaf and blind,
To touch it with my mind.
And God forgive my pen that mars
His lilies and His stars
And God forgive my strange conceit
To make His rain more sweet,
O pitifully bless the pen
That copies His. Amen.

February Landscape

Here Winter drew the silence like a shawl
About her gaunt grey shoulders; huddling trees
Clawed at the sun with bony fingers; these
With ice grown round them like a steely pall
Were stillborn buds – until the poet came
And grappled death in an embrace so rude

That Spring was born from barren solitude
And beauty crashed down like a living flame.

O happy poet! Could a critic's scorn
Abort the blossom in the pregnant tree
Or slash the sleeping throats of unborn birds
When, beautiful, defiant and forlorn,
You trod the lonely aisles of mystery
And loosed the shaken laughter of your words?

The Poet Walks in April

When I fare forth on April Street,
I wear a tattered garb of green
And shake a crown of silver bells;
Oh, low to shining pools I lean
And preen my feathers like a bird,
I dip and bend and bow and smile
And never mind the sober folk
A-staring at me all the while!

That robin, such a jolly oaf,
Who likes his turf as well as I,
Those simple daffodilly maids
A-curtseying when I go by,
And 'chance some other April Fool,
They're all the folk I care to meet,
For sober sires and stately dames
Are out of place on April Street.

Prelude to Gardens

To plunge my fingers deep in earth
And break its coolness wide apart
Sets free a sudden misfaith
Upon my heart.

O larkspur blue, unborn as yet
Save on the canvas of a dream,
O mystery of cloven frond
And fragile gleam

Of silver from the crimson lip
Of some dew-thirsty thankful rose,
Will you lie lovely on the year,
Who knows – who knows?

You bees that clamber fragrant trails
To stumble, big with treasure, home,
How shall you choose from all of June
My way to come?

And moths like pearly shells washed in
Upon the twilight's tranquil sea,
Will you be here when lilied hands
Ask tremblingly?

So small a thing to lay the seed
Within the waiting soil – but then,
God, the familiar miracle
Of flowers again?

Sir Walter Scott on Memersyde

(*His habit was to stop his carriage on Bemersyde Hill that he might feast his eyes on "the finest view in the Borderlands": on the day of his funeral, the Abbotsford horses, drawing his bier, stopped here of their own accord.*)

Soft then, my bonnies! Here is Bemersyde,
And ye shall rest from the long climb. Your flanks
Are glossy from the body's dew – so rest
And I'll give thanks.
My hills, my purple beauties! What device
Of loveliness have you put on this day,
While Tweed wears on her breast the shattered sun
In shining spray?
I think yon sky that fondles Ruberslaw
Hath sown herself in heather, half in bloom,
Soft-breaking purple bells, the deep fringe lost
In sable gloom.
From Eildon peaks the little people leap,
Shod all in silver, down a rope of mist,
Sharp crag to crag, and swing their chains of pearl

And amethyst.
Ye little liny-whites at your blithesome chant,
Ye ghostie bittern, stark and grim, that stands
In creaking sedge – we are the lords who own
These Borderlands!
The fiery beacon flashing on the brae,
The flinty hooves hard riding through the wold,
Loud-clashing claymores, pibroch in the wind,
All shall be told
In song and story. While the fires still burn
Bright panorama on the lucent brain,
This gnarled hand shall paint till Credit cry
His plaint in vain.

How now, my little ones? The sweet winds tease
Your nostrils to be off. We'll homeward then.
The Shirra hath a task to do ere he
May rest again.

Marketing

Martha-in-Me hurries on with brisk and anxious feet,
Mumbling little homely needs along the market street,
Mary-in-me sighs because the waking day is sweet.

Martha-in-me buys her butter fresh and firm and cold,
Mary sees and falls to dreams of meadow marigold,
Daffodils and honeycomb and pretty things untold.

Martha-in-me chooses apples crisp and round and red,
Mary-in-me bought of scabs, laid down a coin and fled
Because a woman drew her shawl about a baby's head.

Martha-in-me scans the shelves of tempting merchandise
Mary touches wistful hands and laughs in weary eyes,
Martha nourishing her brood and Mary growing wise.

Ah, but at the crowded threshold Martha-in-me glows
Very fierce and valiant for the bruises and the blows
Jostling arms are like to deal to Mary's bargained rose.

A Toast to Pioneer Women

Now, while the wine runs reddest and loyalties leap high,
I give you the dead brave women whose glory will never die,
The dead, brave, wonderful women whose labour and dreams and pain
Nurtured our young Dominion and nurtured her not in vain,
Mothers of Canada – homage to heart and brain!

I give you the fair white fingers, roughened and seamed and torn,
The delicate lovely faces, patient and glad and worn,
The kirtles of snowy linen in lieu of the gold brocade,
The elegant shawls in exile, gallant and patched and frayed,
Mothers of Canada, they who served God and prayed!

I give you the slender shoulders drooped in a lullaby,
And answering the wail of the she-wolves, hushing the hunger-cry,
I give you the thousand beacons of quivering candle-light
Set in the rough-hewn windows to guide men home at night,
Mothers of Canada, keeping the hearth-fires bright!

I give you the little gardens, watered with homesick tears,
The simple knowledge of root and herb, the long faiths down the years,
The aching, dragging, terrible toil that made for a woman's day
And the grim scarred peace of her folded hands when the task was laid away,
Mothers of Canada, broken and proud and gay!

I give you the firm sweet sinew and the broad and shameless brow,
The deep Madonna bosom, the generous Eden vow,
I of the twentieth century, clever and cautious – lo,
I give you the foolish, spendthrift, beautiful women of long ago,
Fuel to the flames that cast eternal afterglow!

Paradox

One can ride for miles and miles beneath a morning sky
With pearl and silver and hyacinth to brush the spirit by,
And only have a record of miles and a road before his eye.

And one can sit in a dingy room with a pencil in his hold
And pipe the little milk-white lambs across a purple wold,
And feel the dawn on the jonquilled hills drench his head with gold.

Yeats Writes His Name

He took his pen and wrote his name.
A thorn-bush crackled on a sidhe,
And one with Cormac's hair of flame
Rose up and told strange tales to me.

As falls a deeply purple bloom,
Dusk fell apart and Fergus' sword
Cut silver stamens through the room,
And Tara's harp flung out one chord.

I saw those hills of fair Kildare
And heard the voice of sweet St. Bride
That charmed the wild wolf to his lair
And wooed the young lamb to her side.

His little oaks made coronal
For Columcille's contented head:
I saw three drops of crimson fall
Where Deirdre's thirsty raven fed.

The boat bears home her three dear loves,
Her falcons three in Death's light boat,
Her song is like the Derry doves'
But oh, it quivers on the note!

I hear wild hooves ring down the hills,
Cuchullain's anguish-riddled steed,
And blood of horse and master spills
More richly than the roses bleed.

The pen falls clattering to the floor.
The vision dies. The long dream clears
And shame and glory lust no more...
And I am blind, of Ireland's tears.

The One Rose

Surely it is the smallest plot
A soul was ever given to tend,
And can it be that God forget
The work I begged of Him to send?

I thought to charm His desert place
To light and sweetness, and He deems
It good that I should learn with grace
To stifle all my splendid dreams.

I use His ancient implements
Of faith and hope – and down the years
My soul, in sight of Heaven, contents
Itself to nurse one rose, through tears.

Who knows? Some pilgrim passing by
This least of all poor gardeners
May see my handiwork and cry
"Lord God, to grow one rose like hers!"

Icarus

A hind with pansy flanks that laves her tongue
By Ghost Lagoon, could tell of birds that ride
The dawn on dazzling wings and dip and glide
White mountain-crests and rose-flushed clouds among,
As arrogant as eagles; and of one
That climbed a breath too far and touched his wings
With sudden flame. Describing fiery rings,
He fell, beneath the fury of the sun.

Ah, broken silver body, thus betrayed
In quest of morning, yours was ecstasy
A thousand shall not know! What heavened power
Panted from wing to wing as unafraid
You claimed the farthest eyrie, proud and free,
And took your fill of beauty one brief hour?

Flower Requiem

I will remember you as joyous things
Growing as tall as Heaven is tall,
Climbing and climbing on your petal wings,
Not dead at all.

I can imagine Heaven-garden set
With row on row of spirit flowers,

Roses and larkspur, phlox and mignonette,
And purple bowers

Of lilac. There will be an angel there
To wander in the perfumed dark
And break a bud, maybe, for her bright hair.
There'll be a lark

For Dawn: and busy golden ghosts of bees
Quaffing deep honeyed draughts; and one
Caressing wind to murmur vesperies
When day is done.

I know there is a flower-Heaven. I know
All sweet spent things will live again,
And you, oh little hurt white bud, can grow
To rosehood then.

Apart

Once, on a wind-blown sweet September hill
These two shared rapture. Half the sunset gold
Was hers, they said, half his. A skylark told
Them equal transport. But a word dropped ill
Between them threw a cloud on either heart,
The singer vanished and the shining day
Turned sadly to the West and would not stay,
And they are old and silent and apart.

Yet she has half of rapture still to keep,
One sunset never tarnished, never dimmed,
One song unsullied by a second tongue,
And he will dream and dreaming, fall asleep
With faith an eager skylark homing hymned
To sunset – years ago when love was young.

Pixie Hoard

Devonshire folk say that the few apples left upon the tree after picking belong to the pixies.

The moon has filled the orchard with her eerie silver laughter,
Old mirth, cold mirth, on frosted blade and spear,

But whose can be the teasing little echoes that come after
And who can toss the tiny bells that tinkle sweet and clear?
Pixies! Pixies! Better not come near!

The shadows in the orchard are spicy and delicious,
Wine deep, vine deep, to tempt the heart indeed,
The trellises of moonbeams are merely superstitious,
For who on shrivelled pipkin or blackened nut will feed?
Pixies! Pixies! Better pay no heed!

Hush! If they should hear you the blossom will be blighted,
Bared boughs, scared boughs, that should have flowered free,
And who are you to leave folks starven and benighted,
Who owns the apples left upon the tree?
Pixies! Pixies! And better leave them be!

He Comes on Kerry

Something in me came home again, came home with eager feet,
And oh, but the Kerry ways were green and the Kerry winds sweet,
And I saw the rose-red fuschia-bells and the soft blue curl of the peat.
The little donkey he let me come, the goat on his ragged tether,
And the wee white sheep on the giant hills in the green, green, darling weather,
The linnet for heaven and I for Kerry wearing home together.

I was born of the far West, but that was all forgot,
For something of me cried out at birth in the warm of a thatched cot,
And milk of Eireann fed my soul, whether I would or not.

I'd maybe slipped from God's care for an aeon or two's space,
But now I was back in a Dingle glen with the tears on my face,
And the heart of me nestled and lay still, like a bird in its own place.

Heroine

She rose up swiftly from the page
As sweet and golden as the morn,
I felt as if the loveliest thing in life
Were born.

She grew, as lilies grow. Love came
And plucked her heart out in the sun.

I felt as if the loveliest thing in life
Were done.

Time tossed the empty husk away.
I laid the book down, closed and read.
I felt as though the loveliest thing in life
Were dead.

Hunter's Moon

I never see the autumn darkly creep
In crimson splendour down the brow of earth,
But I remember lusty men who sleep
Beneath the jealous soil that gave them birth;
This fearful hummock where the elm tree hangs
His mournful banner – does it wall the tomb

Of some proud Indian who loved the tangs
Of this gold month? The sumach's surging bloom,
Is it his blood that dances in a dream
Of stealthy footfall crushing down the fern,

Of nostrils quivering and eyes agleam
Upon the rise where liquid ambers burn
To etch a doe's slim body with her fawn
In dusky silhouette against the dead
Sun's saffron...

Ah, thou bold, sleep on,
The aim long taken and the arrow sped,
But Heaven afford thee stag and sunset hill,
The throbbing carcass on thy shoulder thrown,
And dewy darkling trails, serene and still,
To some celestial wigwam of thine own!

The Seekers

You and I for truth and beauty crying,
Crying from our prison in the night,
Seeking, finding, shouting, losing, dying
To the Light,

Sure of nothing but the hunger burning
For a something better than we know,
Beasts tormented by a god-like yearning,
On we go,

Roused if but a dust-cloud dully drifting
In and out among the prison bars
Clothe itself in gold and take to shifting
With the stars,

Stabbed with longing, sick on lonely duty,
Drunk with restless magic all our years,
Mad to share our wonder, valour, beauty,
Terror, tears,

You and I, so close my little brother,
Comrades of the darkness seeking day,
Strange that we should ever hurt each other
On the way!

Two in November

All the world passed by, the day
The cherry-blossom gathered spray
And broke in beauty soft and white
For the tossing wind's delight.
All the world went hand in hand
Through the Spring-enchanted land
Old folk, young folk, fay folk, lovers
Lambs and birds and blossom-rovers,
Laughing, singing, glorying,
Drank the heady draught of Spring.

Grey the road and silent now
The furrow has forgot the plough,
Poplar trees against the sky
Are knights of darkness riding by,
The shivering, silver pallid sun
Grows old and dies, and day is done.
Creep within and bank the fires,
Stifle all the brave desires,
Draw the shade and bolt the door,
Beauty walks the world no more.

Stay – can all the world be blind?
See what our two hearts shall find,
Fighting through the frost-sweet weather,
Laughing, careless, young together,
Fence and furrow, rooves and hedges
Silhouettes with silver edges,
Branches flashing scimitars
Shouting combat to the stars,
And a glowing hill that sips
Sunset wine with thirsty lips.

While a sad world creeps and cringes,
Heaven shines down in shreds and fringes.

For This New Year

I used to ask, "O Master, make me brave!"
For I was young and hushed and full of tears,
And mirth and beauty tossed aside, and gave
Colossal impact to the coming years.

And now the years are come. And I remember
How sweet the lilac snowed upon the bough,
How leaped the flame before the fallen ember, -
Oh, I remember. I remember now.

My courage was an armour worn to thrust
Off pain. Fool! For it kept out love as well.
I tear it off and fling it in the dust,
My heart cries softly like a wind-touched bell;

"Make me no longer brave, dear Lord – but wise,
Acknowledging Thy love, Thy constant care,
And Lifting to this New Year shining eyes
For anything of Thine that waits me there!"

The Tinker Fairy

I saw the Tinker Fairy on the road this morning,
He was frilling rosy paper for a toadstool shelf,
He had got his hat on backward with the feather pointing forward
And was munching on a mallow while he muttered to himself,

"Oh, it's Tinker, Tinker, Tinker, Jack is waiting for his pulpit
And the clovers must be painted and you've bent the tallest fern,
And please to cut the chestnut leaves more fancy round the edges,
And Tinker this and Tinker that, whichever way I turn!
I've sharpened up the grass-blades and I've tuned the cricket's fiddle,
I've spread the field with buttercups and brewed the catnip tea,
But little I'll be drinking if they keep me busy tinking,
And it's nearly time, I'm thinking, for a holiday for me!

Then "Sir," said I, "allow me. My name is Sam'l Slickspoon,
I represent the company that makes the new machines
For cutting, frilling, hemming, and for planting, seeding, stemming,
Thus affording honest tinkers pleasant rests and in-betweens!"
The Tinker Fairy blinked. Then his cheeks grew very crimson,
He snatched a bulrush cudgel and he coughed a mighty cough,
"This is just preparatory", he announced, all rough and roary,
"To the ending of a story. Now, you vagabond, be off!"
I ran around the corner and I knelt behind a hawthorn
And I laughed to hear him singing, for his song was just like this,
"Why, the fellow must be crazy! Wouldn't I grow fat and lazy?"
Then he prettied up a daisy, and he did it with a kiss.

Forgive me for Remarking
(*A Reprehensible Rhyme*)

I am the Traffic Officer on Conversation Street,
My smile can help remarks across that wobble on their feet,
And shy remarks and quaint remarks and old remarks with charm,
I take a dear delight in lending such remarks my arm.
But low remarks and mean remarks, remarks that anger me,
I take their names and numbers and commit to custody.
I heard someone remark 'She has such laughing eyes,' today,
I knew where that remark belonged and took it there straight-way.
And then I heard 'Her last year's hat' and that remark I let
Alone. It's sitting quite forlorn upon the curbstone yet.
Remarks that lie deserve to die. Quite frequently I shoo
Them into paths of trucks and things and hope they strike them too.
And idle mischievous remarks that run about and hurt,
I try to show them how they spatter cleanly folk with dirt,
But little merry-faced remarks with packages of joy
I toss up high and pat on heads and tell them 'That's the boy!'

And what with Spring and love around and daffodillies out,
There seem so many pleasant things to make remarks about,
If folk will but be careful to be just and to be kind,
Things will, I think, be quite remarkably improved, they'll find!

Convalescent

April says that nobody
Should have to stay in bed,
Anybody may get up
And run away instead,
Far away and far away,
It little matters where,
Any path is loveliest
If April has been there!
You can dig the crisp green cress
Out of bubbling springs
Where baby fishes float
On crystal water-wings.
You can see the muskrat dive
To his reedy nest
While the heron, startled, shakes
Jewels from her breast;
Minstrel vagabonds of birds
Will set your heart aflame,
Gipsy blossoms burst their sheathes
And taunt you for a name.
You can race the madcap wind
Along the morning sky,
The moon will drop you silver quills
To tell the evening by.
Oh, all the magic in the world
Is somewhere just ahead –
April says that NOBODY
Should have to stay in bed.

The Stars Come Out

This is the hour when little round noses
Press on the heavenly window-panes,
The cloud-fleet's in with a cargo of roses,

And day drops anchor on silver chains.
In the blossomy dusk blue gulls uncover,
Startling heaven with plaintive jests,
One circles day like a wistful lover
Scattering shadows out of her breast

Little boy feet on the quay, come slowly,
Little crook'd arms, hold tight your toys,
You that are young and sweet and holy,
Make no laughter, oh, make no noise,
Tides are gathering soft as pansies,
Winds are ripe for the Port of Dawn,
Cut the cord of your golden fancies, -
Now, little star boats, on, sail on!

The Little Ghost of Warwick

Lady Jane Grey was a child at Warwick Castle. At seventeen, having been the unhappy sovereign of England for nine days, she was sentenced to execution with her young husband at the Tower.

Warwick has a little ghost,
A tender ghost no more than seven.
With bare white feet and hair star-tossed
She wanders down the hills of heaven
As moonlight silvers Warwick towers;
It filigrees her quaint full gown
And finds her waist with phantom flowers
All with their green stems trailing down.
Green are the shades in Warwick lane,
The holly leaves shine fitfully,
The ivy links its emerald chain
From yew to stately cypress tree;
Pale rhododendrons hang their bloom
Above the little moon-kissed head
That glimmers in the fragrant gloom,
A child of Warwick centuries dead.
She scatters crumbs to feed the birds,
She comrades with the shy-eyed deer,
The dark leaps softly to her words.
Her baby laughter high and clear.
She climbs the grey forbidden wall

And looks upon the ink-black moat,
And sudden a shadow seems to fall,
A knife of shadow on her throat!
A scream, a swift unchildlike scream
Cries out in terror to the Dawn...

The night turns back to empty dream,
On silver floats a silver swan.

For a Little Boy's Bedside

Let down thy pasture-bars, O sleep,
To please a waiting sheperdkin,
And send thy little good grey sheep
For him to gather in.
He wants to tell the lamkins o'er
And sing his new and solemn song,
One, two, three, four. One, two, three, four.
That he has practised long.

The wind has lullabies to sell,
She leans down sweetly from the sky
And gives each lamb a silver bell
To shake as she goes by.
Come softly now, O good grey sheep.
One, two, three, four. One, two, three, four . . .
Tall Shepherd, bless him in his sleep
Who tends his flock no more.

The Little Beggar Maid

Behold Thy little beggar-maid,
O great and holy God,
Whose feet, all bare and unafraid,
Have dogged Thee down the sun-gold glade,
Who cries within the purple shade
Thy footprints in the sod.

Thy sweet winds dance among her hair,
Thy glory drowns her eyes,
She has more joy than she can bear

If Thou hast left one primrose there
Or strung one bird-note on the air
That blows from Paradise.

Each dawn she cuts fresh cloth of gold
To robe her spirit in,
Dew-rosaries her brow has told,
And warm in her young bosom's fold
The violets scattered from Thy hold
She plucks and gathers in.

All trembling in the starry lane
That winds so close to heaven,
She drinks Thy tenderness of rain
And, 'wildered in her simple brain,
She dreams Thy passion, love and pain,
And binds Thy blood-streams seven.

See now in gorgeous panoply
The cavalcade ride by,
They glow with mirth and minstrelsy,
They laugh and fling her ducats free, -
She begs one crust of bread from Thee,
O hear her lest she die!
O hear her lest she die!

O Singing Heart

O singing heart, shall I surrender thee
Before the rose yield up her living flame,
Before the stars of heaven die out in shame
Or the magnetic moon forbid the sea?

Thou art the fire-tipped blossom in the Spring
Nurtured in secret chambers of the bough,
O trembling bud, must I abort thee now
Who live to an immortal flowering?

Thou art the silver bell, the herald note
Of distant splendours from the climbing lark,
Shall I be mute whose faith might flood the dark
With the full moon of morning from my soul?

One lonely token of the me divine,
One passioned symbol of the holy thirst,
Shall I of sorrow broken and accursed
Dash down the chalice and revoke the wine?

Thou diapason deep of Calvary
That entered me when I was born and takes
My life for ransom when the rapture wakes, -
O singing heart, shall I surrender thee?

In a Valley

I do not know on what unguarded hill
Where all the trees of all the world look on
With quiet joy, Thy heaven-cabin stands
Beneath the blowing pennant of the dawn.

I would not take the pathway, if I could,
That trails the splendid going of the sun
To find the golden doorway and Thy head
Bent over its long task, Thou Shining One.

Enough to reach my spirit's trembling cup
How high to hold the glory of the dew
Thy breath distils, when from the stoop of heaven
Thou callest home the stars from out the blue:

Enough to hear Thy laughter in the wind
That plucks all lutes of branches into singing,
To watch Thy holy impulse lift the birds
And teach the pale young wheat its tawny springing:

Enough, enough, that in the dreadful night
Thy moving candle pitifully shows
The little trustful slumber of the bee
And the unhappy turning of the rose.

To One Mistaking Little Christ

Oh no. This is not little Christ, whom you
Are bringing, smug and studied, by the hand,

This pygmy prodigy, grim lips up-pursed
With epigram they will not understand!
For little Christ is shy and may not be
Paraded. He will come in candle-flame
For Michael; song for Rosamond; for John
The mystic simple splendour of His name.
O cleanly temple of a baby's heart!
O faith full-blown from innocence!
Delight
Will blossom to His footsteps here, and wings
Of soft-fledged wonder startle at His flight.

And little Christ is happy, and will brook
No sober terror in their thought of Him.
He raced the foxes 'cross the hills of Heaven
This very dawn, and shook the swinging limb
For scarlet fruit; threw back His head and laughed
Because the brown owl glowered, and the hare
Dropped to her haunches doubting Him, the young
And shining Hunter, weaponless and fair.

And little Christ is innocent, and wears
No armour. Your stupendous sophistries
Would hang grotesquely on the Child who loves
The iris breaking dew against His knees,
Who rests the lark upon His fingertips
And wears the morning for His pearly crown.
He is the Master Warrior Whose shaft
Is guilelessness. To Him dark hosts go down.
He is the Star of Bethlehem, in Whose
Frail glory mighty planets faint and die,
The young sweet wayside spring for jaded mouths
From bitter chalices, to charm them by.

And little Christ is tender, with a great
Grave tenderness. He broods on beauty dead.
And when, in swift sad sequence, thirty years
Have spent their folly on His blameless head,
He dies for beauty. Think. He dies for truth
And love and beauty.
I conjure you, keep
Washed with humility the hands that go
To waken little Christ from that far sleep.

Mortal

I am so poor a thing at best,
A nameless poor identity,
That none would stay his skyward quest
To feed a flagging zest by me.

And yet – and yet – I am a shell
Of exquisite fragility,
And all the passion of His love
Hath been and left its song in me

And yet I am a crystal jar
Spun out of dew and clarity,
The attar of His tenderness
Hath been and left its scent in me.

And yet I am a star, a star,
Hung high and trembling in the free,
A holy Lamplighter hath been
Hath been and left His flame in me.

A Hill is Only Common Sod

A hill is only common sod
Hungry after God.
She will not let one shadow lie
Between her body and the sky;
She gardens in the dewy hours
Among the sunrise flowers,
And pours out draughts of lilied snow
For beggared little fields below;
She nurtures grave young families
Of strong and holy trees
And sets the throats of birds aflame
To hymn one only hallowed Name;
Oh, proudly draws she down to rest
The night against her breast,
And leans through latticed shadow far
To pluck herself a loosened star.
A hill has splendid quiet scorn
For all things valley-born

And yet is only common sod
Hungry after God.

Sonnet for Night

The door is closed upon the last of the guests,
Turn down the lights and let the music die,
My heart is weary of the day gone by,
Weary of the badinage and the jests:
Unfold, O purple Night, upon my head,
For Day has brought no stars and laughter known
No deeps of music. I would be alone
And climb my stair to sleep, uncomforted.

So, from the merry clamour of my day
Of life, on crumbs of beauty ill-content,
With what strung passion I shall turn away
To feast upon the fuller sacrament
In that most holy Night of mystery
Whose Morning Star shall sing new life for me.

'For My Son
Go, lovely Spring, elusive, tender,
Colouring hill and fen and hollow
With gold and green and sunrise splendour,
But charm me not, I will not follow.

I know the dogwood lights the trail
With crimson faggots, tangled, glowing,
I know the enchanted spot where pale
Sweet violets breathe, and bloodroot's blowing.

And I have heard the alluring madness
Of meadow-larks in search of clover,
I tell you I have none of gladness
To spare so passionate a lover.

O world! O sky! O green earth under!
All joy for me fills one small space
Where God has laid and touched with wonder
A little upturned face.

The Little Boy and the Chickadee

I wish that little boys and birds
Could understand each other's words.
I have a friend, a chickadee,
Who often comes and talks to me
When I am playing in the snow,
I always stop and listen, so
He'll know I try to understand.
I think he's talking of the land
He's been in all the summer-time,
And maybe how he had to climb
A tall pink cloud and slip and slide
To come down on the other side,
And 'bout the fairies over there,
And how he saw a polar bear
And had a ride with Santa Claus.
I know he feels like me, because
One day I said my kind of word,
He looked so startled when he heard
And quickly said, "No, listen to me
And try it again. It's Chick-a-dee-dee!"

The Home-Coming

I've been travelling far – far,
I've seen the airport where planes are,
I've seen them climbing away up high,
Till they almost were lost in the grey sky,
I've seen trains and the railroad track
And engines shunting along and back,
And dozens of cars in the noisy street
And hundreds of people on hurrying feet,
I've seen millions of things and more
And I've come back home and I've closed the door
And asked my tricycle how it feels
And kissed the handle and kissed the wheels
And the seat and the pedals. I've seen the rest
And I like my tricycle FAR the best.

Choosing

The front stairs or the back stairs? Which way shall I go?
And shall I crawl down backwards carefully and slow,
Or shall I hold the finger of someone very tall
And walk down like a grown-up? Or shall I go at all?

The Intruder

Rags-the-Terrier is his name,
Only a week today he came,
But each Toy feels in his anxious breast
That Little Boy Master loves him best.

Oh, it's not so hard for the Picture-Books
That Little Boy Master never looks
Their way; and the Ball perhaps is glad
Of the only rest it has ever had:

The Engine waits on the nursery shelf
And pulls away all by itself,
And a long sleep settles upon the Blocks
Cuddled down in their own snug box.
But over against the bare brown wall,
Staring at nothing, at nothing at all,
A little Toy Dog, his glass eyes bright
With unshed tears, sits day and night,

Wanting a hand upon his head,
Wanting a word that won't be said,
'Cause Little Boy Master's found a Toy
That runs and romps like a little boy!

Measles

I'm shut up in a dungeon and it's high above the street,
So anything – ANYTHING – can happen down below.
There may be milk-white palfreys with shining reins complete
And knights and ladies riding them and laughing as they go.
There may be green huntsmen with silver horns to blow –
How am I to know?

Maybe there's a crier with an old cracked bell,
Maybe there's an ogre (though it may be just a clown),
Maybe there's an ancient dame with lavender to sell,
Maybe there's an organ-man grinding through the town,
Maybe there's a princess with a tall, gold crown –
I can't see down!

Jubilate At Heathrow

I will go straight to Colchester, Camulodunum in the old
and stirring days when Cymbeline ruled the North-East,
as Shakespeare told,
when this green island, split to tribes, primitive, proud,
attuned to war,
still made Stonehenge and lovely things. Blackwater I will
see and Stour
where, in their curraghs gouged from trees, tribesmen had trade
with sea-going Gaul,
and I will look in Colchester long on that great and splendid wall
the Romans built, to mark the place Capital of Britannia, now,
their proud new province to whose weal Britons allegiance true
must vow.
Boudicca, golden Queen, in pride rose up and fealty denied,
slaughtered whole legions; in the end, brought low, leaned on
her sword and died.

On Norman William's Castle roof a tree bids men to heed command.
Within, the small bronze Mercury Romans held God, has lost a hand!
Colchester wove her fame in wool: Churches and monks brought holiness:
at Tymperleys the doctor lived who waited on the good Queen Bess.
Oh I delight in history, though Tacitus would call me fraud
Who only glow with pageantry and leave the moral end to God.

Niagara

Her story is a part of Genesis no scribe set down,
his Eastern world too small
and the forbidding sea his wall.
Look back – no mind can stretch – to the still hour
of God's Creation and the awful power
of heat that must in ice de-flower.

Listen. No sound save silence until blow
the hollow winds that peak colossal snow
blind manless million years ago.
And then that greater light that rules the day
shone and the melted snows rushed down to make,
save where hard rock forbade, valley and lake
and over this rock break.

How many passing centuries have heard
Creation's story in Niagara's tide
while men stand, very small, beside.

February Night

When the wind came into the forest that blustery, blustery night
a star stumbled down in the dark with a light.
The young trees huddled together in whispery, whispery glee,
the old trees never awakened to see
why the floor of the forest should creak with that shivery, shivery sound.
Strange bodiless grey things went dancing around.
Then the littlest tree in the forest grew frightened, frightened, and so
he got right down under his blanket of snow.

Explorer's Jubilate

I thank you for the undiscovered things;
for shy and lovely flowers, wanton wings above uncharted spaces,
trees that keep a proud reserve of beauty, fish that leap, unhurt,
untroubled, in an unnamed stream, hills that are grey and silent with
old dream. For every rich and hidden honeycomb, for every rock that
roofs a busy home of ants and for the green and lazy snake that slides
among unparted grasses, take my gratitude; for all untrodden ways,
undesecrated soil I offer praise, for wasted song, ungathered peace,
and bold uncaptured canvasses of pearl and gold, nothing at all here
of man's devising – a primal curve of earth; a lone bird rising.

To Anyone At Large

You take the rest. I don't care. I am filled with great impulses.
If I could reach them I'd probably toss around stars.

You can take the roses and ribbons and riches and all that
and you take the curtsies and kudos and medals and bars.
Have the moon too and the push and fret of the race for her.
Cold and dead she seems to me in the flame of the art
of two small fists and the trust, the trust in the face of her
who runs with a little girl's cry of joy into my heart.

Seventy

I won't mind being somebody seventy,
little bit tippety, little bit fey,
bobbing the hours around lightly and leaventy,
topply and trippingly, juggling the day,
all the world there for me smiling disarmingly,
ready with elbows and ears and a tongue
and somebody talking of heaven quite charmingly –
could it be seventy's better than young?

Bells

All over the world the bells are ringing,
their glories singing.
From Riverside Church, New York, says one,
"We are the public carillon."
Thousands of people all around
hear our canticled splendid sound!
A chapel in Russia urgent told,
"I am largest. Tons of gold
nobles offered, my bell to build.
Its timbers flamed. I crashed and stilled
and plunged to earth, and was labored out.
I am risen and sung about!"
St. Patrick's bell low murmured, "Stay.
I drove thousands of snakes away!"
Mingoon of India deep intoned,
"The bells of Buddha must be enthroned.
Our clappers are tree-trunks monks recess,
and the deep rich tone is our thankfulness."
A tiny bell in a tiny sphere
spoke for his comrades, sweet and clear.

"We are crotals of Christmas trees
and gay sleigh-bells: we can equal these!
Look to your Bible; Exodus
chronicles folk-lore, yes, and us:
Aaron, the priest, and his story probe;
we hung at the edge of the great man's robe.
From London, that mighty city, then,
speaking to millions, I heard Big Ben;
And Bruges broke out with her special grace,
"We ring for men in the market-place."
All over the world the bells are rhyming
earth and heaven in raptured chiming,
quickening footsteps, charming the ear,
lifting the hearts of men who hear.

For Jennifer Anne

Here were we longing
to have done with winter,
the stern prison of ice
and the pressuring skies
when, out of the fog and the gloom,
she was there.

She was coming and our hearts stirred
and we blinked with the sun in our eyes
and we dropped to our knees, glad and proud
to be taken into the ... old miracle
etched with a sharp new grace,
and I swear
all of Springtime stooped over
and shook at the world to
waken, dance, shimmer,
blossom, carol, shine
down upon this small face.

Padre Island

When the round moon hangs in the Texas sky
Ghosts go walking the Gulf's grey shore,

Ghosts of Padre from years gone by –
Spaniards tossed to her sandy floor
From wind-ripped galleons pouring gold –
Laughing savages gay to kill –
Fair daughter of Ponce de Leon – bold
Hunters, men with reckless will
To blaze new trails to the storied east –
Zachary Taylor's Texas Rangers,
Each man urging his brown beast
On to the Mexican land of strangers.

Look to the Gulf. In the moon's cold stare
Ghostly craft on the ebbtide drift –
Natchez raft, poor desperate dare –
Dugouts of Indians deadly swift –
Ingram – pirate of England he –
De Soto, burning to lave his tongue –
Sieur de la Salle with his fleur-de-lis
And hundreds of heroes still unsung
Commend them all to His patient care
Who pitied and loved and held them there
And the servant of God, his priest who came
And gave the island its tall proud name.

The Odd Little Soul

I

My soul is a very awkward shape. It does not settle down comfortably within me. It bulges, tilts and staggers, may not be taken comfortably into crowds, and yet cries out that it is a hard thing to be solitary. In my bigoted adolescent days, I thought of souls as static things and, dismayed by the goblin absurdities of mine, I planed and whittled at knobs and sharp corners, all aglow to make it symmetrical and shapely like its companions. I wanted to confine it into a neat little, conventional frame, and I achieved that by chopping it off at heel and toe, like the ugly sisters in Cinderella. The trouble was that the effect of this salutary disciplining, like the effect of Alice's magic-shrinking mushroom, went on and on. From the accepted pocket-standard size, my soul continued to peter and dwindle, growing pallid, skimpy and dismal, until at last it settled like dry bones inside me.

One day, then, shyly, I opened the door and let it go free once more. It was ridiculous, clumsy and ecstatic, drunken as a long-legged lamb in its first clover. I was almost pitiful of it and had no heart to call it in again. So it grows and runs wild among the daisies, children and sunsets; has Daedalus' wings and loves to climb beyond its strength; has the elephant-child's 'satiable curiosity and pries; has Pan's velvety larynx and laughs aloud and often. And it is (like most of its kindred, I now suspect) host to a good many queer, battered, and dogged, little hopes – and kneels.

It is odd about souls. One is apt to shut one's own up in a small corner of shadow somewhere, a little ashamed that it is timid and secretly doubtful, and has fantastic terrors of its own, while other souls are keen and rapturous, lusty for the next episode in the Great Adventure. It must be true. You can hear their laughters blown back on every wind. They have caught even the clawed fingers of Calamity and are making her pirouette with them down the days. You yourself would love the warmth and camaraderie, the crush of life, did not a Constant Omen peer and grimace and point a finger at you over shoulders. Pride forbids you crying out, but – does no one else see him? He sobers every fine transport in you, and if he is visible to them, they are all indifference.

Well, but did you not read your Invitation to Life, then, this hour of unbearable splendour? It promised, you remember, flower-scent, singing violins, warm beating hearts, red wines, deep glances. And, very small, down in one corner, it told you, "Masks will be worn."

II

John Make-a-Dream has been in, to exhibit a steam-shovel Santa gave him for Christmas. Fired by a concert of Hawaiian instruments on the radio, he wrote to the good Saint a request for a "singing harp". The powers-that-be intervened, tactfully insinuating a steam-shovel instead. It is right and fitting, of course, that John Make-a-Dream should concern himself with a pompous, noisy, man-toy like a steam-shovel. Next year, if he remembers the harp at all, he will likely feel shame to ask for it. So furtive a commodity is Romance. John-Make-a-Dream has eyes that are round and luminous already, with the gold of six years' garnering. He will go through life 'contentedly aware of a sort of morning hour upon all sublunary things', and he must expect to be chidden, scoffed at, and ridiculed for his fancies. His fancies, did I say? His faith, rather. And whoso shall offend that faith, 'it were better for him that a millstone be hanged about his neck, and that he were drowned in the depths of the sea.'

John Make-a-Dream and the Doctor, with five months between them, 'are college pals'. This is their own designation, and the college must have been that joyous fraternity of rattles and feeding-bibs, whence one graduates with so swollen an importance, to Very Young Manhood. The Doctor is cheery and forthright. He pins his fancies down to earth and worms the best out of them. He knows, even thus early, that physical pain is a literal thing, and one pushes his small nose hard into it and doesn't whimper. The Doctor came home 'shoulder-high' from his lonely battle with poliomyelitis a year ago. I could not go to battle with him, but for six months I was as close as war lets love come.

His room was crowded, even in the beginning, - the big, iron splint that took the little leg into its strangely tender keeping; all the soft-colored, paper birds we could lure inside, fluttering from wall to wall: whole engine-yards full of trains; Pooh Bear and Waddles, the oil-cloth duck, and Neddy. The day before the Doctor went away to battle, he had recited, importantly, in the living-room, the 'pome' about Neddy, the 'best little donkey that ever was born', and Neddy was there, waiting his return from the Hospital, and waited on, patiently, (like the little good ass on which Maid Mary and Baby Jesus rode, before Bethlehem) the six months a little boy needed his stout and cheery, equine personality by the bedside. The room was crowded, even in the beginning, and by six month's time, our two astonishing souls, the Doctor's and mine, simply reached out, overflowing themselves, and grew together in comradeship, like twin gossamer bubbles from the same clay pipe.

The Doctor has grown robust and merry now, and carries his steel brace nonchalantly, as a gentleman should, his medals. He is brusque and superior to blandishment; but times, in the fearsome part of the story, or with the day growing tired, I can feel that staunch, little soul of his lean up against mine again, as, in the first days of his fighting, mine, at the lonely outpost, leaned on God's.

III

Miss Sagacity keeps her bed this morning, flushed of cheek and heavy of eye. Hers is a minor malady, but highly infectious, for every occupant of the nursery shares her symptoms. Robert's healthy, Christmas-doll complexion (Robert is a lady) takes on a hectic tinge, and she seems alarmingly rigid of arm and leg. The Bath Salts Dog hangs out inches of furred pink tongue. Pause, the Cat, has no spirit to lick his whiskers. And Raggedy Anne's wide grin has a glittering, Christian determination about it, and yearns, I am certain, to be taken off and laid away to rest in a drawer somewhere, with no responsibilities.

Miss Sagacity once declared, in a moment when her small stomach fairly creaked with a burden of chocolate bar, gum and ginger pop, that she was really little tempted by such things. Dark was capping her 'big day' and sleep was imminent. 'I just love my bed best' she avowed, with a wide declamatory sweep of her hand, 'God and Jesus and then my bed'.

She is a small dynamo in her daytimes, and a comical sophist at times. She told us one breakfast-hour that she had tried hard to go dead for a minute in bed, 'just to feel it'. She had, she alleged, succeeded in getting her breath stopped, but her heart "beated on'. Nay, little Miss Sagacity, Death's a solemn gentleman and will not come merely to be peeped at. And yours is too little and too gay a figure to be walking the long corridor yet. It is an out-grown fallacy, and you must not think it, that one dies and goes to Heaven to find God. He is there, indeed, but Heaven is a chartless territory and has never been surveyed. And, what with every January twig outside your window dripping a silver fire, and a child in a scarlet coat making soundless music with a hoop, and the smoke from countless hearths curling up, like blown feathers from swan's breasts, into the blue beyond, and a black and white and blood-red bird (the colors Deirdre loved) making a xylophone of the apple-tree – why indeed, Miss Sagacity, I do think with the poet 'the whole round earth is a God-filled place'.

IV

This is one of those chill grey days, heavy with suspended rain, that are become so many in our Canadian climate. They are not lovely to look upon, except as backgrounds. Consider (as the Red King says, in Wonder-land) the chaste, quiet loveliness of trees, communing in those cathedral skies: the green friendliness of plants clustered in cottage windows; how beautifully laughter kindles, in the drab street; the lively mushroom crop of flowers that bloom ruddily in windows, to light lovers home; and fi-nally, in the blue dusk, the stars.

This day is the very home of English roses, reddening in exiled cheeks; of bewitching tendrils of hair, curling under coquettish caps; of five o'clock firelight, delicately dancing tea-cups, innocent gossip and camaraderie. It is a regular Feast of All Souls, peopled with friendly, little grey ghosts stepped out of hearts and hearths and book-shelves. There may never, indeed, be quite such sweet and homely intimacy again.

Polly Comfort, in her rose-colored coat and cap, comes plump-ly down the street and is met by the General Manager, whose demure, heart-shaped face, with its fringe of brown hair, tied into a quaint brown bonnet, somewhat belies the astuteness of that young person's charac-ter. Polly is as rotund as a little girl can comfortably be, and has a large dimple in each cheek. She is one of those tantalizing, small mortals who invite kisses, and do not greatly care for them. The General Manager links paws with her and they disappear in the direction of the playroom, immediately deep in jargon of concerned parent-talk, pertaining to dol-lies' ailments. The General Manager's dignity is somewhat marred by her constant and delicious perversion of all "r" sounds. She adjures her child to go to sleep 'like a good ge'l, for Muddeh' and adds with artful persua-sion that 'all the little bo-dies are snug in their nests by now!'

I confess to a deep and abiding joy in Make-Believe, myself. I am not one of those females who clasp to their hearts and apostrophize as 'ador-able' any small, appealing object, from a bisque doll to a pet monkey. But I do shamefacedly acknowledge that a wishful-nosed Teddy Bear, priced three dollars and a half in a Christmas exhibit, was almost too much for me; and if there be no audience to listen and stare, I can talk solemn nonsense with a child for hours on end. I tell the truth, to the best of my ability, to the little 'faces looking up, holding wonder like a cup'. I have heard the fairies 'all among the limes, singing little fairy tunes, to little fairy rhymes – lots and lots of times'.

The General Manager, swishing a junior-sized duster with all the energy and none of the usual disinterestedness of four years in such domestic operations, observed suddenly, 'It's all right for Jock to go to Gamma's House today, Muddeh. Next time I see him I'll just shoot him!' She was as calm as that, in the face of a great calamity. Grandma's House is the Treasure Island for all seven of these young mariners for adventure. It is spacious and sunny, inhabited by curious Grown-ups, and has mysterious caves and crevices that invite happy investigation. One puts into cheery harbor there, scouts around and sniffs for 'citing things, (the Doctor's expression) and after an hour or so of this delightful exploring, when the shouts of 'All aboard that's going aboard!' one carries away, in one's small paddy, a bag of loot, to ease the pain of parting. Indeed, there is difficulty at times, in persuading the crew to weigh anchor at all, and, on occasion, near-mutiny; wherefore we have pinned up, conspicuously, in the dock-yards, the following suggestions in etiquette for out-going craft,

The Way To Leave A Grandma's House

Is lonesomely but brightly,
And wanting very much to stay,
But going quite politely.
You might just tell the Teddy Bear
(He's quite bowed down with sorrow!)
That if he eats his porridge up
You're coming back tomorrow.
It's best to let your clothes get on
Without a bit of scriggling,
It makes galoshes ornery
To find their feet a-jiggling!
You might just stop and tell the fire,
'Toast Grandpa's feet. Don't burn them.
If he should close his eyes a bit,
He might forget to turn them!'
It's best to go and say to Cook,
'The supper was delicious.'
It makes her think of pink ice-cream

And nuts in shiny dishes!
If Grandma's cheeks are somewhat round,
You might remark, and kiss one,
'The King-of-England's Grandma's House
Is not as nice as this one!'

V

A voice is heard yodelling, rather expertly, from the floor below. With the sound of the voice comes another sound, a muffled scratching, interspersed with the pad-pad of small trotting paws. I dash out of my den (where I am supposed to be in a state of literary coma, unconscious of the outside world) and put my head over the stairs, in time to see a bluff and braw young gentleman, about the size of the General Manager, and a small, white, Aberdeen terrier, disappear into the playroom. The yodelling continues from behind the closed door, and is punctuated, at times, by a shriek from one of the little maids, on whom Jock is exercising his masculine prerogative to tease.

Jock should wear the kilt, and have none but heathered hills to walk upon. He has even the Highlander's weathered, muscular knees. And the Aberdeen terrier would be so joyous with a little loch to wade through (any blonde-complexioned canine gentleman can do with a loch or two, usually, for perfect ablution!) and golden gorse to rub his nose in, and ferrets, to plague out of their subterranean tenements and harry across a moor.

Jock's mother, who is only one or two sizes bigger than himself, was born in Ayr, within a few rods of the Ploughman Poet's Brig o' Doon; and Jock's paternal ancestors swung their dark tartans in great numbers, on the roads converging at Dunrobin Castle, when the pipes disturbed the silences of the Highland hills with their 'Pionaireachd nan Catach'. Their badge was the red-berried Butchers' Broom and their motto (d'ye hear this, Jock, latest-born of a proud line?) 'Sana Peur'.

The Aberdeen terrier suffers, with all the usual gallantry of the small dog to his master's whims, the extravagant caresses that must be anathema to his middle-aged and rather staid spirit. MacPhee has a cat's luck with his life. He mislays himself, times without number, and says his dog-rosary to Heaven, beneath the wheels of countless trucks and bicycles; and on the morn's morn, you will meet him (or his bathed and curly ghost) taking his customary zestful trot out on the Avenue, in excellent fettle for further adventures.

He looks on, with the anxious, unwilling interest of the Elderly and Experienced-in-Such-Things, at Jock, earnestly turning forbidden taps all over the lawn, and hurtling his small body out of reach of the spray, with fiendish delight. But MacPhee has the supreme necessary attribute of the perfect playmate – He Does Not Tell.

Jock has mercantile leanings, and delights in dispensing wares, preferably delivering them in trucks, with ear-splitting sirens and in need of constant repairs. He has a service-station in his own right, and enjoys being hearty and highly efficient for applicant motorists. He sells buns at a thousand dollars apiece, and spare tires at ten cents a dozen. He will deliver any commodity to any district, the hillier and muckier for wheels, the better. I once heard him petition Heaven fervently to 'deliver us our evil' and imagine he has visions of it arriving, with much snorting and shouting, at the tradesman's entrance, in crates and packing-boxes.

Dear little Jock! He will know one day that the markets for bartering material things are situate, chiefly, in Stupidity Street, and that only from the mint of his own clean soul comes the shining currency that has power to obtain for him the 'loveliness Life has to sell'.

VI

Then there is the Born Agitator. He precipitated himself, like a charged missile, into my den today, filled with impatience, because it is his birthday and he is no more of a success than this time last year. He combed his hair so often and so wildly, with his smouldering pipe, that I had to propel him gently into a chair at last and soothe him with quantities of sugary tea. My den is small, and it is necessary to move some of the furniture into the hall when the Born Agitator visits me, he has such long and emotional legs. I have known him to wave a whole chair aside, with his foot, when he was discarding one of my feeble, feminine comments from the discussion.

"I am No Good,' he pronounced, dejectedly, sky-writing with his pipe, with a fine disregard of ashes on the rug. 'I may as well face it. And now another year's to be ground out. I do hope ___ "

I took down a worn, little, red book from my shelf. "Bah!" I snorted, cutting short his eloquence with unfeeling, "You are only good to 'chase swallows with the salt'." (By this time you will have discovered that I am rather fond of Stevenson.) The B.A. put his boots up on my pet cushion and looked resigned, and I read from Virginibus Puerisque, 'Hope is a kind old pagan; but Faith grew up in Christian days, and early learnt humility. In the one temper, a man is indignant that he cannot spring up, in a clap, to heights of elegance and virtue; in the other, out of a sense of his infirmities, he is filled with confidence because a year has come and gone, and he has still preserved some rags of honour.

We celebrate our adult birthdays, methinks, with too much private tremor. I am not yet grown fond of Browning's bland conjuration to 'grow old along with me, the best is yet to be'. That is too much for hot-blooded youth to swallow, all at one reading. The physical and the spiritual are too closely bound up, and we cannot be taught, but must discover for our own exigencies, the peace of the twilights, the riches of memory, and the audacious joy of crying Sesame, at the closed doors of the Kings' Treasuries.

But, dear Lad, I am convinced that the quest, itself, is all that matters, and the astonishing truth that at any moment the painful blunder, that warped grey root, may split a sheath, and blossom suddenly into one's Best. I dare to think, too, theological dogma to the contrary, that it was not Jesus Christ's humility that made His death on the Cross so glorious a gesture, but His splendid arrogant faith in Himself, despite the Sanhedrim, as the Saviour – the Saviour of mankind.

Something of all this I said, in my stumbling fashion, to the Agitator, and presently had the satisfaction of seeing the bent corners of his mouth straighten out, and even take on a little upward curve. (The B.A.'s mouth remains very 'baby' and must have an unhappy time of it, between his rugged nose and exceedingly stubborn chin.) I suspect it was the sedative effect of my voice (which the B.A. likes) and the sugary tea, rather than my pearls of philosophical wisdom, that had the desired effect, but at any rate he was in quite a softened and penitent frame of mind, by the time the sandwich-plate was empty, and ready to admire my profane arrangement of the Bethlehem pilgrims on the cake-plate, being three gingerbread ducks (the Wise Men) following a star a-sparkle with candied sugar, and off in one corner a skeptical Humpty Dumpty, battling a Mephistophelian citronpeel eye upon the scene. All the Wise Men disappeared, and the B.A. liked them, for they were full of spice.

He departed, looking quite uplifted, and patting me on the shoulder with lordly, male condescension, not unmixed with gratitude. He is very loveable, the Agitator. I shut the door after him and looked around, sheepishly, at all the grinning faces on my walls. I love my little den. I would be very hard on an interior decorator's morale, for the White Rabbit, with his kid gloves and fan, looks as if he were heading straight for the Rose Window in Rheims Cathedral.

"I know," I admitted to him, humbly, "I am a humbug. Only last night, I was whining that the wine of life was gone sour on my lips, and cherishing a rich taste for the hemlock-bowl ___"

"O my ears and whiskers, how late it's getting!" he replied, irrelevantly, and hurried off round a corner.

<h2 style="text-align:center">VII</h2>

He was nine years old, and very pink and scrubbed, I am sure, in the middle of him, under the blue pullover. Only his boots and his brown lanky paws were mostly muddy, because a football is. He smelled of scent, though, and it was a good strong, man-smelling scent, like burned leaves and tar-paper and butternuts and spy-apples and fish-worms. He read, but was not especially keen on it, unless the page was blood-spattery. He liked to tramp and play and whistle better. And he liked houses.

Houses were living, to him. Every one had a personality. His mother's was little and low and comfortable and shabby; really a grandmother's house, with a bonnet of wisteria and lilac, and a plump, white bosom, buttoned all down the front with little clumps of Johnny-Jump-Ups and Lad's-Love. Everything about his mother's house, the poplar trees and the little, dappled hen-mothers clucking in the sunshine, the grey cat blinking out of her amber spectacles and the orchard grass, silky with dew, sang lullaby. His mother's house rocked by an open window of clover and musk-roses, and at dusk wrapped itself in ever so many fleecy cloud-shawls and went to sleep, as the doves in the dove-cote told it to.

He remembered his baby resentment of the Townley House on Teller Street, with its broad, red, staring face, its insolence of bold, green awnings, its flaunting porches and pillars, and lamps smirking from windows too near the street. Poor, well-meaning Mr. Townley had got together all his money with hardly more than one sweep of his blunt, grimy and hearty hand; and most things he did, offended, his house most of all. The little boy forced himself to saunter past it, on his morning route to school, with an indifferent air, and it got in his way and made faces at him.

But there was the Rookery (where the Rector's wife lived in her enchanted garden, and talked of God as John Make-a-Dream does, with happy matter-of-factness); and the Apple-Pie House with the fork-marks all over the plaster, where the Old Woman in a Shoe lived, with her eleven children; and pleasantest of all, there was Come Awa' Ben, 'out of the wind's and the rain's way', where Granny MacGregor gave him oat cookies and buttermilk, and kept house for her fine fat pig and her chastened, wee 'guid mon'. Oh, he loved houses!

One day it stormed, and he had a sniffy cold. Idly leafing through a magazine of his Mother's, he found a poem called 'The Empty Little House' about a little house, just the sort he could see in his mind's eye, the sort you could love, that had lost its tenants. He read it through, and then he read it through again, and both times a horrid, big lump came in his throat, and another settled, like a rock, in the pit of his stomach. It went like this:

> Nobody ever stops to see
> What flowers grow in there
> Nor if the lilac tree is out,
> Nor what the windows wear.
> And oh, the little house must look
> As if it didn't care!
>
> No fingers ever lift the latch
> Of such a rusted gate,
> Nor footsteps hurry up the path,
> Afraid they might be late,
> And oh, the little house must act
> As if it didn't wait!
>
> And when prospective buyers come
> And poke about and peer,
> And cry their caustic comment on
> The hallowed things so dear,
> The broken little house must smile,
> As if it didn't hear!

And all that dismal day, and the next, when he was feverish, the little House haunted him. He could see it so clearly, little and dear and built for happiness, wearing so plainly its hurt, forlorn look of having been left alone, like an old, forsaken woman, with its hands empty.

Quite late that night, he asked his Mother for a pencil and paper. He chewed the pencil a long time, and frowned and struggled. Then he began to write terrifically, as if his life depended on it, as maybe it did.

After a bit, his Mother smiled, because she heard distinctly a key turn in a rusty lock – and a fire crackle – and a baby crow.

'But now' (he was writing) 'a family comes to town,
The windows all wear lace,
They've built a roaring fire upon
The empty fire-place,
And so the little house is glad
And wears a smiling face.'

His mother wrote me the story of this, addressing me in the care of the magazine, after the little boy slept that night. She said she hardly needed to read what he had written, when he handed the page to her.

But of course she did, because she loved him.

VIII

Your legs would not go. Your heart went, on double time. Your body shrank and dwindled to the diminutiveness of Hop-o'-my-Thumb's. Your head swelled and rocked, like a diabolical Jack-o'-Lantern's. You conceded now, that they were right about there being 206 bones in your body. You had that many aches. All that day, you gravitated between fear that you were dying and (like the seasick sailor) fear that you weren't. You slept at last, fitfully dreaming that you were tossed about in a sluggish ocean, your feet tangled in iron chains of seaweed.

You woke, cooler, and very tired. So tired that you stayed in bed, to rest, for nine weeks. The hot-house roses in your vases changed to fat, little pots of pink hyacinth, with its 'years' at the Spring fragrance. (How you envied Pippa her dancing feet!) Whole armies of stout pussywillows, in grey fur busbies, marched in and took possession of your dressing-table. Easter lilies hung their white bells, with the golden clappers, from your windows. The Doctor (the little 'tend Doctor, as he called himself,) came and laid over you a consoling manly arm. (When you are vertical, he is just as high as your heart.) "Well sweetheart," he drawled, sympathetically, "I expect you'd just like to frow yourself in the garbidge?"

Then the first morning came up in pure gold, and the dark, tossed plume of spruce that filled your window and had kept company with you all winter, matching its mood to yours, was all fringed and frescoed and filigreed, combed through and through with gold. The squirrels chivvied along the fence, full of the news of April. You heard a robin chuckling his

'Thank-You-for-rain' song, between tugs at his squirming and resisting daily bread. A muddy-mittened, little fist brought a handful of hepaticas to your bed. You asked for a pencil and scribbled across your tempera-ture-chart ' _ all the magic in the world is somewhere just ahead, and April says that NOBODY should have to stay in bed' and left it, looking plaintive, where the Big Doctor would see it. He was an understanding person, the Big Doctor. He didn't frown when you insinuated, hopefully, at the foot of a page of temperatures, 'Saturday, the same as Friday, cross my heart, and hallelujah, praise the Lord, there's no more chart!' Nor did he essay comfort, when you idiotically burst into tears one day, out of a clear sky, and without a hanky.

Violets came, a big, round bowl of them, and you remembered

'Such a starved bank of moss
Till that May morn
Blue ran the flash across,
Violets were born'

And decided that you would like to farm, not ducks, pigs, corn and 'taters, but – violets. A violet farm. The miraculous purple, and black-shadows-in-purple, of it! The sweetness! People would laugh at you – but your world, with the sun in it, would be a gold-and-purple, royal banner, pinned across your beast with the Golden Arrow, and you would walk with 'a mort o' bees and warmship, and want nought of any man.'

The weeks dreamed on, and the little door of your heart opened and shut, lazily, like a warped dyke against a slow floodtide. Then, one morn-ing in May, you opened your eyes, and there stood in the doorway with the shy smiles of having found you in sleep, John Make-a-Dream and the General Manager, cheeks pink as apple-blossom, eyes round with delight of the new morning. You reached out your arms and lifted them up, one on each side of you, on the bed. Something strong and warm and sweet pushed through your veins like an elixir. Was this how Jairus' daughter …?

"In the littlest house with the verandah on it _ " began John Make-a-Dream.

"A bo-die _" went on the General Manager.

"Has put some eggs _ " took up John Make-a-Dream.

"And we _" you dared, breathlessly, and wriggled your toes free of the blankets.

"Will go and see them!" finished everybody, crescendo.

So you did.

IX

Mr. Woolly is third of the little Doctor's family, having followed along (as who would not follow?) on the heels of Polly Comfort. He is rotund and rosy, too, and his whole life is centred, it seems, with a passionate devotion, on balls.

"Was ever," questions Mr. Woolly, wordlessly, with his wide blue eyes complacently sweeping his small horizon, "Was ever world so enchantingly and magically furnished with balls?" One sucks them (until reproved) on the tops of bed-posts, digs them out in fascinating orange overcoats, full of pin-pricks, from bins in cupboards, bounces them happily into paths of oncoming Persons-with-Dishes, jostles them experimentally on Christmas trees, until they fall off the stems and shatter into a hundred brightly scintillating fragments.

'Ball' thus far, is Mr. Woolly's entire vocabulary, and were he verbal, would express his compendium of the joy of living. To be sure, he did meet a Ball once (a vulgar sort of fellow he turned out to be) who promised all kinds of fun, being the lightest, airiest and bounciest playmate, and wearing a waistcoat of the most delicate and ravishing azure-blue. One carried this fellow to a Grown-up every now and then, and the Grown-up applied his mouth to the Ball's ear, and blew a terrific blast of air into him, and the Ball quivered with mirth, and grew larger, rounder and jollier every minute. To what mad dimensions he might have it within his power to grow, Mr. Woolly could not guess; but the Grown-up having tied him (the Ball) very tightly around the neck and bounced him into the air, Mr. Woolly gave up trying to imagine, and bounced after him in high glee.

A wild game ensued. The Ball led Mr. Woolly a merry dance; he (Mr. Woolly) dipped, teetered, staggered, churned the air, and finally sat down, with great suddenness, on the floor, and let forth peal on peal of open-mouthed mirth in frank appreciation of his own antics. At the very peak of his enjoyment, the Ball lighted, surprisingly, against a sharp corner of the radio, promptly emitted a terrible and blood-curdling oath, and expired; whereupon all the little up-curled curves on Mr. Woolly's face froze on the instant, slowly untwisted themselves out of laughter, and curled themselves up tightly in the opposite direction, in a fearful howl of pain and disillusionment. Balls, then, were not immortal. This precious, azure-blue and spirited one was no more. A torn and sodden thing of rubber lay on the floor, and Mr. Woolly could not make head nor tail of it, much less ball. He kicked his sturdy heels, in a lusty rage against Fate and the universe and all who tried to comfort him. He refused to be comforted.

In the midst of the turmoil, the door appeared to push itself open, and a pumpkin entered, followed by the Doctor, his face wreathed in smiles. "From Gramma", he announced gustily, "For a punkin-face. Daddy kin make it. And pie!"

Mr. Woolly unscrewed his eyes. Incredulous joy spread itself over his moist features. He stood on his head, and balanced himself on his four little paws carefully, for an instant, preparatory to rising. Then he set out, purposefully, for the Doctor, and reaching him, wound his two arms with proprietary affection about the object of his desire. Beautiful world, that shattered illusions, only to provide newer and more delightful ones! Beautiful, luscious, round, golden gift-of-the-gods, this 'punkin'!

"Ball!" proclaimed Mr. Woolly, from a full heart.

X

I have been telling the seven, lying on the grass in the sun, the story of the Little Red Hen. Mr. Woolly, to be sure, is not listening, because he is experimenting with dirt as a viand, and finding the experiment highly interesting. I shall stop him if he begins on a worm, but, for the present, let him revel in it. I suffer from a savage form of dirt-hunger, myself, in the Spring. I envy the very hens that scratch in it. I envy the 'young green corn its springing' from the earth, and the white roots that distil their bitter juices in it, and drink from it again.

It thrills me to know that I am a flower sprung from the soil, created from dust, vitalized by breath from the Divine nostril! The first-fruit, in very truth, plucked in the primal, golden harvest. I am guilty often of merely murmuring a form of prayer, with half a mind on it, but when I have sinned, and am stricken, and creep back to the Almighty knee, black and foul and festering, crying 'God, be merciful,' I pray as Saul Kane prayed, for the heavenly ploughshare to cut its deep, clean furrow through my soul, and turn out the black-rot to purge itself in the blaze of His sunlight, and leave the soil sweet with potential corn, quivering with a premonition of lilies.

'O Christ who holds the open gate,
O Christ who drives the furrow straight,
O Christ, the plough, O Christ, the laughter
Of holy white birds flying after,
Lo, all my heart's field's red and torn,
And Thou wilt bring the young green corn,

The corn that makes the holy bread
By which the soul of man is fed,
The holy bread, the food unpriced,
Thy everlasting mercy, Christ.'

There is a great cry abroad among the skeptics, of the day of Miracles being done. It is a fantastic conclusion. I would not, indeed, have the courage to subscribe to it. True, the modern miracle is not wrought as dramatically as in New Testament days. Jesus Christ knew that His ministry on earth was to be brief, and must be colorful and vivid to accomplish its purpose. But the miracle of the loaves and fishes happens over and over again in these half-famine days, and Love is still, as it was then, the distributing factor.

Science has its explanation for British dominions matching greetings on Christmas Day, across the intervening oceans (the poignancy of that pregnant moment between the old Chief's hearty, ringing 'Hello Toronto', and the youngster, with a hot sob in his throat and not going to be caught at it, smartly clicking his heels: 'Hello ... London!') Science can explain the television, that is in process of perfection. Science is silent on what a flower, a sunrise, a phrase of music, can and does do to a man's soul. Science is God, with a finger to His lips, protecting man from himself, preserving him wonder and hunger and that 'divine discontent', setting a part and beyond him His mysteries of grace, that the ancient quest for Beauty may still go on.

I travelled once, by train, through the Annapolis Valley, when the manna was spread out there. Every tree, miles upon miles of them, hung to the ground under its burden of luscious fruit. Suddenly the doors swung open, and the train, that had been hot and smoky and foul with the taint of many breaths, filled from end to end with the sweet scent of apples, the rich harvest of the crimson year; the fulfilment of the delicate promise of pink and white apple-blow in the year's May-time, when 'fifty-Springs' seemed 'little room' indeed, for wonder.

That is as near as most of us come, I suppose, to the miracle itself. We catch a drift of its light, color and fragrance. And we eat, complacently enough, of its fruit. So Life goes on, and the prober in miracles grows 'perplexed, and spectrepale'. Not all his 'weary lore of sleepless nights hath power to touch, like one low daisied sod ... We are but child-kin to the birds and grass and he who yearns, life's heir, and kin to God.'

But what is this? A goblin, drawing his sword on a giant's territory? I take up, dreamily, the forgotten thread of the story. (It is high time, for Mr. Woolly has made great headway with the dirt.) "Then I'll eat it myself," said the Little Red Hen. "And she did."

"Gosh, she must've got a terrible pain, eating a whole loaf!" commented the Doctor, feelingly.

An appalled silence fell on the seven. This was a possibility that had, hitherto, not presented itself.

Then the General Manager stepped in to meet the situation. "Her muddeh fixed it!" she asserted, with cheerful finality.

XI

A child, at bedtime, takes on a sort of unearthly, brilliant beauty, as if it hovered, fragile and ethereal, like a butterfly, on the fringe of the flower of sleep. Few things relinquish their fierce, little intermittent vitalities so gracefully. A street lies empty and forlorn between sun and star time. A house wherein no occupant is, to light a beacon in the window and kindle a fire on the hearth, to throw its red and friendly gleams on the drawn shades, receives night sullenly, even morosely. Screaming hawks wheel over forests, and bats are born, with velvety-soft bodies and sheathed talons, out of sinister shadows, and blot out laughter and sereneness and melt back into shadows again. Dark is ominous with possible disaster; crime and disease have their haunts and breed in the terrible No Man's Land, between day and specific day. And Sleep, like a good mother, comes with stealthy footsteps, and waits long and patiently, exercising her gentle ministry, before she has her reward of the unclenched fist and the smoothed forehead. Man is born, and dies, on the defensive.

But a sky, a bird, a bee and John-Make-a-Dream accept the dark beautifully, and give themselves, full of radiant faith, unto Night, her keeping. With the sunset, John Make-a-Dream clothes himself in every possible splendour, his cheeks brilliantly crimson, his hair rumpled gold, his eyes deepened from blue to a lustrous iris-colour. Like a vesper-thrush, John-Make-a-Dream bewitches himself into the most melodious, mad laughter and song; and like a bee, he becomes, at last, sweetly top-heavy with drowsiness, and tumbles into his blankets and tucks them about him like the petals of a fresh rose, and is suddenly still.

John Make-a-Dream takes his treasures all to bed with him, an excellent habit, providing they keep their places and do not grow unbearably glamorous and disturbing, as one's treasures are likely to do against the background of the dark. A fire-truck, a picture post-card, a tattered, but indomitable, wool puppy (his shrill bark carefully and courteously suppressed, though no sign of sleep clouds his bright and penetrating glass gaze) stow themselves o' nights, in the warm valleys-between-the humps of John Make-a-Dream's bed, and he has been known, on occasion, to waken in the faintly rosy dawn and protest their removal. Quite right, John Make-a-Dream! The treasures that are ours of the dark, who dare take it upon himself to disturb? My daytime deportment belongs, in a sense, to my jealous world, and trembles beneath the jurisdiction of many eyes. But my dreams in the dark, the property of my soul, the dear, little furniture of my mind none moves, dusts, polishes and caresses but myself alone. What a slight issue is communism that pertains only to matter and material things! God carries the keys of the soul's archives, and will discover the contents only at love's behest.

John Make-a-Dream, Miss Sagacity and the Doctor will go to morning church, soon. Even the General Manager has been, and derived an infinite amount of entertainment from the clergyman's gesticulations during his discourse, and from the novel spectacle of Persons Not in Sleepers and Meemonas, praying together in daylight and in public. Before these small worshippers learn to sing, how I should like to delete from the hymnal such loose, ugly and forbidding phraseology as 'Death's cold sullen stream' and 'the dread hour' and 'the dark vale' ...

I am not unaware of Death. When it robs me of what I love, of my poor humanness I shall go uncomforted. To the customary barren condolences, I shall answer, with Edna St. Vincent Millay, "I know. But I do not approve. And I am not resigned."

Yet, when my own hour comes, I think I may go as the bee goes into the rose, all faith and simplicity, and There bide, in the joyous knowledge of perfect tenderness and perfect beauty all about me, for the first time in my consciousness. If there be an emergence from that rose, how breathlessly lovely it promises, for, as the bee assists at the marriage of the flower, so will the soul have been told of God's secret of eternal life, and will come forth at dawn to the garden again. All radiantly golden with the very pollen-dust of immortality.

XII

I have been reading to the little Doctor from the Household Tales of the Brothers Grimm; and I caught myself indolently wishing, for one moment, that life might be as simple as one of these fairy stories, for the little Doctor's living. A goose with golden feathers in return for the sharing of his crust of bread, a wishing-cloak and a winged steed for his courage, precious jewels for his fidelity to duty, and a beautiful princess (oh, a beautiful princess, little 'tend Doctor!) to marry and live happily with, ever after.

But the very next breath I drew was one of hot protest. Life as simple and smug as that, only a jigsaw puzzle to be fitted together, according to design, for the little Doctor, who only last year, convalescing from poliomyelitis, loved to ring his stout, little challenge down the long hall, to welcome visitors to his bedroom:

'Brave Admiral, say but one good word,
What shall we do when hope is gone?'
The words leaped like a leaping sword
'Sail on! sail on! sail on! and on!'

He learned "Cargoes" too, and liked to startle unsuspecting grown-ups launching 'quinquiremes of Nineveh' with a relishing roll of his small tongue. He listened with still delight to Robin Hood's 'ghostly bugle-note shivering through the leaves' and screwed his eyes up tight, declaring he was 'tending Sherwood Forest'. He bore the 'chicken-pops' with admirable fortitude – fever, vaseline-baths and all – because Hiawatha wrestled so valiantly with the Spirit of the Corn; and he applauded, fortissimo, the announcement of his shivery morning scrub because his Peary, his hero, had never flinched from cold or discomfort.

About this time the birds began to figure largely in his interest (one of the most inspired hours of bird 'reminiscences' and bird-song Stuart Thompson ever gave, was given in the little Doctor's room one evening, prior to the naturalist's engagement, under Kiwanis auspices, to an audience of several hundred) and he took story-time out of his nurse's hands, one morning, and narrated a thrilling yarn of a fictitious voyage of Peary's that he had 'dreamed'.

"The ship", he recounted, vigorously, "suddenly goed bang! crash! Into a pink iceberg and splitted it in two, and Peary hurried 'n put on his swim-suit 'n jumped in 'n lifted up the iceberg, and underneath it was – what d'you s'pose?"

I averred my utter inability to guess, splashing on the rubbing alcohol with suitably animated recklessness.

"Downy Woodpecker", revealed the Doctor, impressively. "Dead. But Peary got him alive again, of course!" Of course, Peary was capable of any, even a superhuman achievement.

I had a pair of loop ear-rings. Of good size and pleasing shininess, and the Doctor frequently wore these, with a beret dashingly over one eye, and was blood-thirsty and terribly profane in conversation, being the

'-Pirate Don Durk of Dowdee,
Who was wicked as wicked could be,
But oh, he was perfectly gorgeous to see,
The Pirate Don Durk of Dowdee'!

With Tinker-Toy equipment, we made a cage for the 'parrot called Pepperkin Pye' and hung it from the electrolier, by a gay red ribbon; and the Big Doctor bumped his head on it when he came, and the little 'tend Doctor' grinned, and flourished the dangerous weapon known as the 'squizzamaroo'. Oh, those were brave days, indeed!

And how, pray, would the adventurous spirit of the little Doctor fare, oh foolish one, in a lotus-eating sort of world, where rewards hung on every tree, for the mere pleasant picking of them? I heard a little story that grew out of the depressed financial and trade condition of the times. A little lad broke his toy, and said, "I'll make a better one from the pieces!" The task took all his wit, grit and endurance, but the toy made a pretty fine thing – out of the lad.

What riches of the spirit has the little Doctor, (or Don Durk of Dowdee) stumbled upon, already – the fine gold of courage; the rubies of good cheer; the white pearl of patience; the gleaming silver knocker on the door of the King's Treasuries!

He used to sit, later, by an open window, in a room full of open windows, muffled up in coat, cap and mittens, and swing his red, yellow and green balloons afar and wide, for passersby to see and wonder at. The cheery Chickadees and Yank-Yank, the nut-hatch, and Redhead Woodpecker made heyday for him, and he laughed and grew hungry for supper, and rosy of cheek and nose. But he was not meant to sit by and look on at life. He was meant to join step with the March of Souls.

'Allons!' (then, little Doctor) 'after the great
Companions and to belong to them!
'Forever alive, forever forward,
'Stately, solemn, sad, withdrawn, baffled, mad, turbulent, feeble,
    dissatisfied,
'desperate, proud, fond, sick, accepted by men, rejected by men,
'They go! they go! I know that they go, but I know not where they
    go,
'But I know that they go toward the best – toward something great.'

XIII

A car slid up to the door of Grandma's House. Out stepped Jock, in white flannel shorts and a silk shirt-blouse. Out stepped MacPhee, with the look of one Recently Bathed. Out stepped Lorna, who is Jock's faithful playmate and companion. Out stepped Jock's Daddy and Mother, and Jock's other Grandmother. "We slept", announced Jock, to the assembled grown-ups on the veranda, "in a cabbage."

Suppressed mirth from Jock's parents, who explained that they had week-ended, for a 'lark', in tourist cabins by the lake. Any mind, but a goblin mind, would have inferred that, immediately. The goblin mind, however, did actually entertain for one brief instant, quite a delectable vision of rosy, little Jock, like a very sturdy and blooming fairy, asleep in the cool heart of a giant cabbage, with layer upon layer of fluted, green satin, billowing and curling around him. A slug must own it very paradise in such an environment, though someone wrote once, I remember, of a kitchen garden.

'And the cabbages, the fat, stupid cabbages, spread,
Their vacant features, in a sleep they have not earned,
Dreamed again of the white butterflies, who had said
Such faithful things last summer, and never returned.'

How one word (even so homely a word) has power to work witchery in one's brain! Do all writers, I wonder, suffer the nightmare of words beautiful, wild chaos (has chaos a plural?) of words, tumbling through one's consciousness in a very Niagara of silvery thunder, in the deep hours of night, when all should be tranquility? Oh, the mute and terrible paralysis of the fingers that would pin them down in permutations and combinations of poetry! Oh, the unsung songs! The unbuilt temples! The unsown gardens! Surely, all beauty is cradled in one warm, glowing hollow between the stern prop of reality and the shining pillar of the dream: and faith is the twin in the cradle.

> 'Good, good it is to dream, for dreams
> Are beautiful in God's sight,
> The spire that never rose to gleam
> In any but the mind's sunlight
> Was spun of rarer gold. The hand
> That set the bulb in earth, that minute
> Raised up a bluer hyacinth
> Than earth had ever cradled in it.'

A child's experimental manipulation of words is deliciously humorous, though the humour will scarcely bear relaying in the clumsy, self-conscious hands of the adult. A wise grown-up keeps his laughter at childish blunders in his heart. It is sweetening there, and does no hurt.

The General Manager presented herself at my desk, the other day, and requested me to make pencil-sketches of the various persons and things. The one of Uncle Bill (my talent for art is definitely a minus quality) was especially ludicrous. Uncle Bill was leaner and longer, even, than the original, and the fore part of him seemed to be getting somewhere, much ahead of his legs and feet. He presented a fairly good impersonation of a gentleman about to be sea-sick. The General Manager gazed at him for some minutes, in silence. No adjective in her vocabulary of four years' collecting, seemed adequate to this masterpiece. Then, in a burst of illumination, she remembered a word Grown-ups occasionally use, with good effect. "He looks," ventured the General Manager, with some uncertainty, "Ang-sceeous – angscous – Anxious."

She waited, quite breathless with suspense. I could feel her small body rigid against me. (Please God, make that the right word!) "He does look anxious", I agreed, with conviction. All her breath escaped suddenly in one happy sigh. She gave me one of her infrequent, fierce kisses. "I love you!" she avowed, passionately.

Well – I remember a little girl who wrote a story in her mother's recipe-book, at the tender age of seven. It was a lovely story, done in ink with curly tails and capitals. It wound up to a grand finale, with the information that the 'hero walked away with the air of a Bronchitis'. What? You never heard of that stamping, wheezing, roaring, snorting animal, the Bronchitis, first cousin to the Jabberwock? Then you have ridden all your staid and pitiable life on the tram-cars of conversation, and know only the travelled routes. And there are thousands of dear, of charming, of lovable, of nonsensical words that are to be gathered from daisy-fields, and plucked off gooseberry bushes, down-the-lanes and round-the-corners! You may never find the happy by-ways now. A long, long time ago, you must have forgotten to take the Wrong Turning.

Last Spring, one of the little Doctor's little wrens flew about, fussily, without a mate. A grown-up friend asked him if he knew what the word 'bachelor' meant. "Oh, sure!" replied the little Doctor, intrepidly. "A bachelor is a person who goes about talking a lot, and thinking a great deal of hisself."

XIV

The wind, my goblin brother, is abroad tonight. He has a giant's stature and vigour, and can seize the tall pines by the hair and shake them properly, and ruffle the snow-lace on the broad brows of mountains. But he is a very goblin by disposition, spending his energies in prankish, droll and impractical ways, and with a strong taste for eery (sic) haunts and elfin pastimes.

A very good fellow, indeed, to be out with, he will do me the most beautiful turns in the matter of bloom in John Make-a-Dream's cheeks, and stars in Miss Sagacity's eyes. He thinks nothing of climbing trees, and tossing down armfuls of bronze-and-gold leaves and sweet, red apples, for a child's delight. He blows (obligingly) little, rude paper boats down miniature streams, slaps the pavement smartly with ripe chestnuts, and cries 'Boo!' at them, when they one and all curtsey to nothing, with a sort of surprised, but determined, homage. He delights in feats of strength with Mr. Woolly, who, even heavily freighted with layers of blue crocheted armour, and supported by two excellent, fat, little legs, is still Easily Blown Over. And he babbles in the little 'tend Doctor's ear, of kites and balloons and sailboats, and makes him, by his own confession, "cited."

The wind is a genius of sorts, and a versatile fellow, too. I have seen his long fingers weave in and out among the snow, fashioning the most exquisite, flawless sculptury of lilies and of angels. I have seen him point his brushes and paint the most delicate flesh-tint friezes, from a palette of apple-blossoms, on a wall of blue sky. He has moulded the liquid silver of river-water for my delight, and mounted in it pearls and diamonds, and, by moonlight, opals, for Night to wear on her dark, velvety bosom. He brings me phials of precious scent, from rain-washed narcissi or nicotania. On a June night, if he wake at all from his drowse of beauty, he goes drunken with the garden's attars. And every swinging branch and tinkling leaf and deep-strung guitar of a partridge wing, is his instrument, from which he strikes his tender, weird and beautiful melodies.

But do I keep my indolent chimney-corner and refuse to go frolicking with him, then he plagues me at doors and windows with a very devil's tattoo of imperious tappings, ghostly whines and wails, and groans like a hunted banshee, until the cold perspiration breaks out on my forehead, and my teeth ' 'gin a-chattering'.

And when the fire in the hearth dies down, and is only a tired, soft mass of congealed smoke and turquoise embers, when the long shadows are asleep on the wall, when the heroine of the tale has been roused and loved and broken, and time has tossed the empty husk away, and I have 'laid the book down, closed and read, and felt as if the loveliest thing in life were dead,' – then does this wind, crying his solemn requiem about house-tops, seem to have caught up into his ghostly keeping, all patient and resigned, passionate and bitter sighs, from the lost breath of the great and noble company of the dead, and let them loose, a dark and terrible torrent, upon such of the world as are awake to hear them. Dr. Johnson, the big, imperturbable man, defeated at least in the death of his loved wife, by the one force too strong for him, conjuring the 'Governor of heaven and earth, in whose hands are embodied and departed spirits' to make him responsive to Thy government'. Keats, of the 'singular beauty and brightness', with a golden bugle ready to his lips, sick, scorned, desperate in the throes of a triple passion, 'cowering under the wings of great poets', the candles ... burnt down ... using the wax taper', Charles Lamb, sacrificing his life to the care of a pitiably demented sister, and laughing off the sacrifice: (nay, he would be angry at me for the use of the word); only by candle-light and shadow sitting alone (with a thin wall between him and her delirium whom he loved) and wondering, as a child wonders, on life and 'lachrymae rerum'. De

Quincy, covering the waif-child's misery and loneliness and terror with the valiant rags of his own. Happy, unhappy Hazlitt, who rode the compass of a star and sickeningly crashed into his own soul at the completion of the orbit. And that forlorn and wistful poet who penned, by the pale beacon of his candle, in the stillness all alone, a strange paradoxical letter, to be delivered 'a thousand years hence':

I who am dead a thousand years
And wrote this sweet archaic song,
Send you my words for messengers
The way I shall not pass along.

I care not if you bridge the seas,
Or ride secure the cruel sky,
Or build consummate palaces
Of metal or of masonry.

But you have wine and music still,
And statues and bright-eyed love,
And foolish thoughts of good and ill,
And prayers to them that sit above?

How shall we conquer? Like a wind
That falls at eve our fancies blow,
And old Moeonides the blind
Said it three thousand years ago.

O friend, unseen, unborn, unknown,
Student of our sweet English tongue,
Read out my words at night, alone:
I was a poet, I was young.

Since I can never see your face,
And never shake you by the hand,
I send my soul through time and space
To greet you. You will understand.

O goblin wind! Are you a purveyor of souls' intimacies?

XV

Janet Muffin looks after the household accounts. This task should really be mine, and by all the rules of logic, I should be excellently well qualified to perform it. I have divers imposingly inky diplomas in a drawer, somewhere, to vouch for my capabilities in the science of numbers. I have even mounted a platform, and expounded on mathematics (in their primary convulsions) before lackadaisical juveniles.

Despite all this, I am chronically confounded by figures: and what I call overlapping subtraction, where the article is priced sixty cents, and myself not having the exact change, the salesman glibly suggests that if I give him a dollar and ten cents and he returns me two quarters, we will be 'square' – this has been known to keep me half an hour late for an important engagement, and give two persons (myself and my 'opponent', whom I instinctively mistrust) headache.

But anything I suffer in these slight dilemmas ls nothing to the concentrated agony of Janet Muffin, over the weekly budget. Belying her name, this good soul is long and angular, with a resigned mouth, and competent spectacles, which I think she must have been born with. I found her this morning in her favored (of necessity) establishment, at the library desk, with a large, imposing tome and several of its children grouped in front of her; also ink (red) and ink (blue) after the manner of Christopher Robin's geraniums (r.) and delphiniums (b.) and a pen and ruler. She looked up, alertly, at my entrance.

"It's the charities, column 3, page 9, that put me out," she explained, confidingly, as if we had just been interrupted and she was taking up the thread of the discussion again.

"Do you call them that in the book, Janet?" I accused. "What a horrible habit, like chronicling sunrises! I thought they were a sort of – well, of love-affair, that went unspoken and unclassified, except according to heart-beat."

Janet Muffin put on her endearing, little, troubled look. "What would you head them then, Miss?" she enquired ingratiatingly.

"I shouldn't," I responded, flippantly. "I never heard of any book-keeper in the New Testament entering up his loaves and fishes. What a muddle he would get into, to be sure, when the five became five thousand and fed the multitude and left a balance! No, Janet Muffin, one column in my ledger would just remain a blank, and then whatever I was out in my final reckoning I should know really belonged there."

But there'd be a Deficit!" objected Janet Muffin, in a reverential tone.

"I know, and I should simply write in below it with sublime Christian faith, "The Lord will provide.""

Janet Muffin sniffed, disparagingly. Then she remembered her grievance. "Well, it's them puts me out," she reiterated, plaintively. "I no sooner get them fixed into their proper places, Humane Society into Humane Society, and Missions into Missions, and beggars at the door into Transients – than somebody takes Humane Society to pieces and puts it all on a new system, and Missions gets itself divided into Home Missions and Foreign Missions and Special Collection and Thank-offering (what's the good of all those pigeon-holings, anyway?) and I'm all kittersnatcher again!" (Janet Muffin's vocabulary is subject to no dictionary restraints.)

Miss Sagacity appeared in the doorway. "Gramma says she wushes you will please write a cheque for the oil-man: and Fancy needs some more milk-tickets; and Gramma took some bill-money from the drawer, for the apple-man's little girl that has a sore heart again, but you needn't put it down ..."

I laughed. "You see, we're two to one about Column 3, Page 9, Janet Muffin," said I. "You'd better dispense with that column. No self-respecting ledger owns to one."

Miss Sagacity advanced to the desk and placed her chin on the grandfather tome. Her two large, bright, brown eyes fixed themselves earnestly on Janet Muffin's face.

"And there was a Poor Man came to the door, hadn't had anything to eat all day, even not any brektus, and Fancy gave him some sandwiches and some change-money, and Grampa said he'd been thinking it over very seriously, and he'd come to the conclusion that he didn't want those things keeped track of in a book ..."

Janet Muffin jumped to her feet, banged the desk shut, and Flounced off. Her face was pink, and she sputtered incoherent exasperation. Miss Sagacity, with her born histrionic aptness, swore lustily on her behalf.

"Oh flapdoodle!" spoke Miss Sagacity, blasphemously, and vanished in Miss Muffin's wake kitchenward.

XVI

"Twitter-Twitter!" says a small voice from the apple-tree, unmistakably, however, a human voice. "Twitter-twitter! I am an oriole."

I am enticed to the window. On a low bough of the apple-tree is perched the little Doctor painstakingly humping himself over into what he imagines to resemble bird-contours, and gazing down, with a bright, commanding eye, on Miss Sagacity, below. Miss Sagacity is on her knees in the mud, assiduously searching for worms.

"Lady," the Doctor addresses her, experimentally, "I want some string and mud for my nest, and you have to help me tie it up like a basket!"

I close the window, softly, not to disturb their precious 'Tend'. How often have I only set foot on the miraculous Borderland, and breathed its sweet, enchanted airs, and heard the Nightingale, from its hawthorn glades, telling me melodious 'Well come!' when suddenly a door has slammed, a bell has rung, or a voice jarred down on my senses, and that green vista of 'Tend' has vanished into the Never-Land, to the end of time; since 'Tend' is a land of a million toll-gates, and never opens the same one twice!

With what tender eyes must God look on little children at play in the green valleys of 'Tend', all the world over! How He must turn to such a sight with gladness, from the sick distempers and sated follies and sophistries of His grown children!

I never walk in country places that I do not come on God, chuckling over some bit of His handiwork. His humors, as sweet and candid as a child's, are everywhere – in the burls and knots of forest trees, in the infant acorn on the stout oak, and the gourd on the delicate tendril of vine, in the droll waddle of a duck, and the studious lantern-face of a frog by the brook's edge. I know that He turned the first sticky, whiskery butternut over, in His hands, with a boy's pleased laughter; that He bends branches into ridiculous sharp angles and purses up His lips to whistle through them o' nights. I know that He walks abroad in April, tenderly mirthful at the crowing of the cock (yes, Peter, with mirth that has 'no bitter springs'); at the rooting of the red sow in the trough, with all her clumsy, gluttonous babies, like burrs on her mud-caked flanks; at the round-eyed, silly trout hanging themselves in a sort of silver ecstasy on the most obvious gallows, rigged up of string and bent pins, and gloated over by a small late disciple of Isaac Walton's. (I think God loves all fisher-folk. I think He knew that James and John, the sons of Zebedee, had, of their chosen livelihood, a culture not imparted in schools, but closer, perhaps, to the hungers of men. Who lives between sky and earth in all weathers and 'seeks his meat from God' has, perforce, to follow the simplest faith in the world.)

There is a poem of Katharine Tynan's on the making of birds, which says, in part:

'God made him birds in a pleasant humour;
Tired of planets and suns was He.
He said "I will add glory to summer,
Gifts for my creatures banished from me!"
He had a thought and it set him smiling,
Of the shape of a bird, and its glancing head,
Its dainty air, and its grace beguiling:
"I will make him feathers," the Lord God said.

The dear Lord God of His glory weary –
Christ our Lord had the heart of a boy –
Made Him birds in a moment merry,
Made them soar and sing for His joy.

How close you are to Him, little children! I can hear your laughters blended with His, together.

The Born Agitator read this, and asked me, hesitatingly, whether I had ever felt doubts of the quality of His laughter. "There is this in the Rubaiyat," he added, handing me the little volume open at:

'... after silence, spake
Some Vessel of a more ungainly Make:
They sneer at me for leaning all awry!
What! Did the Hand then of the Potter shake?'

I turned the little book over in my hand. Such beautiful poetry! Such bitter philosophy! "I think," I said, slowly, "It is a very callow and a very rare one among the Vessels that sneers. You may have noticed that the Grecian Urn only continues her quiet business of being beautiful. Perhaps she is set apart by an ancient wisdom. Perhaps she guesses at God's Law of Compensation. I have never seen Him sneer. But I have known a Pot that leaned awry, and I shall never forget it. Irish Tom Moore knew it, too."

It smelled of roses.

XVII

There is a generous note of scarlet in the little den of which I am so fond. It is a vague promise in the rug, in a sort of sublimated mulberry, drifting through the blue. It becomes bolder in the flowered cushions; kindles all manner of seductiveness in the dark leathern jackets of books;

makes a pyre of the Waste Paper Basket for all little, dumb martyrs of Rejection Slips that perish for the faith; flows in a silken tassel from a paper-cutter; glows in two candles on Grandmother's carven, walnut brackets that flank my desk, ___ but comes, triumphantly, into its own, in the little, red, china Figurine who promenades, daily, the book-shelf just over my head.

What a darling damozel she is, to be sure! – in scarlet flounced petticoats over a modest hoop, a jacket of watered silk over a tight basque, fastened with a cameo, a wide-brimmed black hat (Gainsborough?) with a drooping feather, and the inevitable, scarlet parasol, shading a delicate skin and blonde curls from the sun's too fervent kisses. The hands that twine about the stem of the parasol are incredibly white and gracefully shaped for no more demeaning labor than, perhaps, 'to sew a fine seam' or to flutter a wisp of a foolish lace handkerchief, beneath a honeysuckle arbor, after some reluctantly departing male figure.

I love this little lady. She is so poised, in a world of futile gesticulating. She is a very Vestal Virgin, who keeps sanctuary. And yet she is deliciously warm and alive, and knows secrets, and has given her lips, or I mistake, to love and to laughter. She is the composite type of all lovely women, from Cleopatra: and were she to exhale breath from that sweet bosom, one magic evening in the candle-light, what tales she could tell!

Tell me, then, did you sip circumspect tea in Cranford, oh small Scarlet One, and take an elfin delight in shocking Miss Matty, with your coquettish furbelows and glances? – dear Miss Matty, who was convinced, you remember, that 'Marriage is a very solemn thing!' Are you, perhaps, impersonating that 'kind, fresh, smiling, artless, tender, little domestic goddess' of Vanity Fair, whom men adored and certain women 'saw through'? Were you one of the gay company who gathered in the famous old Hall of the Middle Temple, to dance Sir Roger de Coverly with the gallant gentleman himself, or to look on at those earliest produced Twelfth Night fantasies of Will Shakespeare's? Did you – oh, did you, little Scarlet Lady? – preen your curls and dissemble your provocative blushes for the naughty benefit of the ogling Mr. Pepys, three rows behind you, resplendently conscious of his new periwigg, at the King's Playhouse? Surely, then, 'my lady Castlemaine' must have looked to her laurels!

There have been marvels of discourses carried on by the sages, in this small room, under your tiptilted nose, oh Scarlet Lady, to which you listened with your lips curved in a gentle mockery. But when the door shut on the last departing guest and I stumbled back to you in the blue haze of smoke, with my hands outstretched, pleading an answer to all their questions, you dropped your eyes, still with that sweet enigmatical smile on your lips, and Would Not Tell. Ah, well! That is the prerogative proper to your charm. You have a right to be mysterious.

Over the fence of a tall book-end, my Scarlet Lady was wont to peep, with shy delight, on John Galt's Parish people, busy at their homely activities: but one night, chancing to look upon Milady Macadam, at her endless picquet, and being quite withered under the keen surveillance of the old lady's eyes, she came to me in some trepidation lest she had been guilty of offending one of the large family of Little Ghosts, to whom she is sister. Seeing her so prettily discomfited, I immediately busied myself in meddling a bit with topographies on my desk, and have her much happier now, in the gentle, if discursive, company of the Professor at the Breakfast Table, along with Iris and the Little Gentleman, who have expressed only mildest and friendliest curiosity regarding her family background and personal affairs and predilections; and possess the inestimable charity in all their theoretical hypotheses, of Making Allowances.

XVIII

John Make-a-Dream gazed with some admiration on his achievement, a small be-thumbed water-color sketch, wherein three real pussy-willow cats, with long, inky, gracefully curving tails, sat firmly (aided by glue) on a sky-blue fence, eying a mournful moon. I was beside him.

"I think," said John Make-a-Dream, aglow with the slight lunacy of the creative artist for his new-fledged chick, "I think the queerest thing in the world is when you say, 'You can, John,' and then" – his words resolved themselves into radiant capitals – "I CAN!"

It is, John Make-a-Dream. The queerest and most beautiful thing in the world. The clear oil that lubricates all spiritual machinery. The bright magnetic Star. The cup of cold water to parched lips. The strong hand beneath a trembling elbow. The corner-stone to every temple. Gardens. Ships. Songs. Love. Hope. God. The One Thing Left.

From my early morning bed, I carry laughter into my day, because the eyes and lips and hearts I love are looking for it. Am I brave? Am I true? Am I loving? It is your good faith in me that demands it. Does my presence sweeten, strengthen, stimulate? Does my hand achieve great things? Do I lift up my voice and sing? Do I make great laws, voice great wisdoms, avert great catastrophes? Not I, but this mysterious, unutterable, unfathomable, incomprehensible mystery of your faith in me. My faith in me. Mine in you. Ours, together, in God.

The mother works miracles, by faith, in her child. The wife, in her husband. Friends in friends. Lovers in lovers. Nations (God teach them!) in nations.

John Drinkwater, in his play 'Abe Lincoln', puts into the mouth of Abraham Lincoln's wife on the eve of her husband's Presidency, a homely and stupendous utterance. She says, "They're coming to ask him to be President, and I've told him to go. I've watched and watched, and what I've learnt, America will profit by. There are women like that, lots of them. But I'm lucky. My work's going ... farther than any of us can tell."

Faith, the handmaiden of God, drives a beautiful, mad chariot, that stops nowhere this side of heaven. Superb in her strength and stature, her glorious eyes alight with the hunger of aspiration, she tosses her golden voice to the four winds that blow, in a mighty challenge. "Own no boundaries, see no bars. Here are lilies – but there are stars!"

The possibilities within me, no man knows; the sleeping powers, no man dare estimate. Are you my friend? Believe in me.

The saddest words in the whole epic of Holy Scriptures follow the assertion on the lips of the most marvellous Personality of all time, in His home town of Galilee, that 'a prophet is not without honor, save in his own country, and among his own kin, and in his own house'. And he could do there no mighty works. Bitter must that cup have been, as the very gall on Calvary. He, the God-filled Man, in Whom all things were possible, to feel that rich power waste out of Him, because His own whom He loved, withheld their faith from Him. Pale-conscienced cowards, afraid to gamble on the most Glorious Game in the annals of history!

My tongue stumbles, over the Apostles' Creed. I shall never be quite glib with it, for it professes greater things, almost, than one soul can take care of. We of this generation (I want to be one of them), John-Make-a-Dream and the Doctor, Miss Sagacity, the General Manager, Jock and Polly Comfort, Mr. Woolly and I – we are going to be more careful, please God, of our professions and our pretences at wisdom. It is a sad thing not to see God, but it is a sadder thing to see Him only because we stand in a place of vantage and, in our deliberate gross and smug selfishness, shut out the view of Him from those who stand behind.

We are coming into our inheritance, and lo, it is a broken world. So fine a thing it seemed before, and so glittering close the ball spun to the giddy peak of fortune, that we thought to do without faith, and we flung it away and trod it with our heels into the ground. Then the fall and the crash and now faith is all the measure between this broken thing, lying at rock-bottom of destiny, and – infinity. Faith and faith's works. Come, John Make-a-Dream. Come, little 'tend Doctor. For dignity, honor, serenity, peace. We will put our small toes to the line and we will recite our new creed, a humble beginning again. 'Lord we believe. Help thou our unbelief!'

Perhaps the queerest and most beautiful thing in the world will happen. Perhaps, from Faith's far Somewhere, a cry will sound, a Divine cry, exultant ringing, vibrant through all the vaulted chambers of the mysterious heavens, deep and passionate with great joy and great love – "You can."

For nothing is, or will be, of which God and a soul, together, are not capable.

Eight Haiku

Delicate new moon
how can you have ocean tide
at your beck and call?

Croak, frog. Wag, goat's beard.
Hop, cricket. Good donkey, bray.
Laughter has virtue

Crows chatter somewhere,
My head hangs. Is this still cheer
or scorn of man's ways?

Wind, you have playthings,
my hair and scarf and raincoat.
Two feet refuse you.

The rounded pebble.
Turn back a million years now
to hear its story.

Small knobs of cherries,
larks from the thrusting clover-
stir, stagnant blood. May!

Black sky, you threatened
the earth with deadly missiles –
this is a snowflake.

I painted nothing.
I was lost in wonderment
at God's canvasses.

Epilogue

There it is, the story of a happy rhymer
whose liveliest period was half a century
back. Then there was no sales pitch. I need
only make an audience happy, or write – pure
joy, even now, for
Anne Sutherland Brooks

ACKNOWLEDGMENTS

Many thanks to Sarah Brooks, Elizabeth Walker, Martha Brooks, Jeremy Luke Hill, the University of Guelph McLaughlin Library, and the Guelph Public Library.

ABOUT THE EDITOR

Edward Butts is a graduate of the University of Waterloo, and spent eight years teaching at a school in the Dominican Republic. He is the author of numerous books, including *The Desperate Ones, Running With Dillinger, Ghost Stories of Newfoundland & Labrador, Wartime: The First World War in a Canadian Town,* and *The Mad, Bad & Dangerous: Volumes I & 2.* He has been nominated for the Arthur Ellis Award for true-crime writing, the Red Maple and Hackmatack Awards for juvenile non-fiction, and the Architectural Conservancy Ontario Heritage (Media) Award.

He lives in Guelph, Ontario.